| Tibet

Titles in the Genocide and Persecution Series

Afghanistan
Argentina
Armenia
Bosnia
Burma
Cambodia
Chile
Darfur
East Pakistan
El Salvador and Guatemala
The Holocaust
Indonesia
Kosovo
The Kurds
Liberia
Namibia
The People's Republic of China
The Romani
Russia
Rwanda
South Africa
Sri Lanka
Tibet
Uganda

GENOCIDE & PERSECUTION

| Tibet

Jeff Hay
Book Editor

Frank Chalk
Consulting Editor

GREENHAVEN PRESS
A part of Gale, Cengage Learning

GALE
CENGAGE Learning·

Detroit • New York • San Francisco • New Haven, Conn • Waterville, Maine • London

Elizabeth Des Chenes, *Director, Content Strategy*
Cynthia Sanner, *Publisher*
Douglas Dentino, *Manager, New Product*

LIBRARY OF CONGRESS CATALOGING-IN-PUBLICATION DATA

Tibet / Jeff Hay, book editor.
     pages cm. -- (Genocide and persecution)
   Summary: "This title explores decades of conflict and violence in Tibet, with historical background, an examination of the controversies, including the assertion that China committed genocide in Tibet, the status of religion in Tibet, what outsiders have done in regard to Tibet, and personal narratives of those affected"-- Provided by publisher.
   Includes bibliographical references and index.
   ISBN 978-0-7377-6901-2 (hardback)
  1. Human rights--China--Tibet Autonomous Region. 2. Genocide--China--Tibet Autonomous Region. 3. Political persecution--China--Tibet Autonomous Region. 4. Freedom of religion--China--Tibet Autonomous Region. 5. Tibet Autonomous Region (China)--Politics and government--1951- I. Hay, Jeff.
   JC599.C62T5378 2014
   951'.505--dc23
                                                                    2013031892

Contents

Chapter 1: Historical Background on Tibet

   Alex McKay

   A writer examines Tibet's long history as both a power in Central Asia
   and a target for such empires as Britain and China. He also touches on
   Tibet's isolation and unique forms of social order and Buddhism.

   Encyclopedia of Modern China

   The troubled and complex relationship between Tibet and China goes
   back at least as far as the early years of China's Qing Dynasty (1644–
   1912), when Chinese authorities sought to assert their control over the
   region.

   Government of China

   After China absorbed the independent state of Tibet in 1950, claiming
   that it traditionally had been part of China, leaders of both regions publicly pledged further cooperation in 1951 based on a seventeen-point
   agreement.

   James Steinberg

   An author describes how China tried to assert its authority over
   Tibet in the 1950s and how Tibetans saw many Chinese measures as
   heavy-handed, staging a major rebellion in 1959. One result of the

unsuccessful uprising was the departure to India of the Dalai Lama, Tibet's spiritual and political leader.

Supported by their spiritual leader, the Dalai Lama, Tibetans protest against alleged attacks on their culture in the months before the event that Chinese leaders hope will be an important showcase for their country.

Chapter 2: Controversies Surrounding Tibet

Chapter 3: Personal Narratives

Preface

The histories of many nations are shaped by horrific events involving torture, violent repression, and systematic mass killings. The inhumanity of such events is difficult to comprehend, yet understanding why such events take place, what impact they have on society, and how they may be prevented in the future is vitally important. The Genocide and Persecution series provides readers with anthologies of previously published materials on acts of genocide, crimes against humanity, and other instances of extreme persecution, with an emphasis on events taking place in the twentieth and twenty-first centuries. The series offers essential historical background on these significant events in modern world history, presents the issues and controversies surrounding the events, and provides first-person narratives from people whose lives were altered by the events. By providing primary sources, as well as analysis of crucial issues, these volumes help develop critical-thinking skills and support global connections. In addition, the series directly addresses curriculum standards focused on informational text and literary nonfiction and explicitly promotes literacy in history and social studies.

Each Genocide and Persecution volume focuses on genocide, crimes against humanity, or severe persecution. Material from a variety of primary and secondary sources presents a multinational perspective on the event. Articles are carefully edited and introduced to provide context for readers. The series includes volumes on significant and widely studied events like the Holocaust, as well as events that are less often studied, such as the East Pakistan genocide in what is now Bangladesh. Some volumes focus on multiple events endured by a specific people, such as the Kurds, or multiple events enacted over time by a particular oppressor or in a particular location, such as the People's Republic of China.

Each volume is organized into three chapters. The first chapter provides readers with general background information and uses primary sources such as testimony from tribunals or international courts, documents or speeches from world leaders, and legislative text. The second chapter presents multinational perspectives on issues and controversies and addresses current implications or long-lasting effects of the event. Viewpoints explore such topics as root causes; outside interventions, if any; the impact on the targeted group and the region; and the contentious issues that arose in the aftermath. The third chapter presents first-person narratives from affected people, including survivors, family members of victims, perpetrators, officials, aid workers, and other witnesses.

In addition, numerous features are included in each volume of Genocide and Persecution:

- An annotated **table of contents** provides a brief summary of each essay in the volume.
- A **foreword** gives important background information on the recognition, definition, and study of genocide in recent history and examines current efforts focused on the prevention of future atrocities.
- A **chronology** offers important dates leading up to, during, and following the event.
- **Primary sources**—including historical newspaper accounts, testimony, and personal narratives—are among the varied selections in the anthology.
- **Illustrations**—including a world map, photographs, charts, graphs, statistics, and tables—are closely tied

to the text and chosen to help readers understand key points or concepts.

- **Sidebars**—including biographies of key figures and overviews of earlier or related historical events—offer additional content.
- **Pedagogical features**—including analytical exercises, writing prompts, and group activities—introduce each chapter and help reinforce the material. These features promote proficiency in writing, speaking, and listening skills and literacy in history and social studies.
- A **glossary** defines key terms, as needed.
- An annotated list of international **organizations to contact** presents sources of additional information on the volume topic.
- A **list of primary source documents** provides an annotated list of reports, treaties, resolutions, and judicial decisions related to the volume topic.
- A **for further research** section offers a bibliography of books, periodical articles, and Internet sources and an annotated section of other items such as films and websites.
- A comprehensive subject **index** provides access to key people, places, events, and subjects cited in the text.

The Genocide and Persecution series illuminates atrocities that cannot and should not be forgotten. By delving deeply into these events from a variety of perspectives, students and other readers are provided with the information they need to think critically about the past and its implications for the future.

Foreword

The term *genocide* often appears in news stories and other literature. It is not widely known, however, that the core meaning of the term comes from a legal definition, and the concept became part of international criminal law only in 1951 when the United Nations Convention on the Prevention and Punishment of the Crime of Genocide came into force. The word *genocide* appeared in print for the first time in 1944 when Raphael Lemkin, a Polish Jewish refugee from Adolf Hitler's World War II invasion of Eastern Europe, invented the term and explored its meaning in his pioneering book *Axis Rule in Occupied Europe.*

Humanity's Recognition of Genocide and Persecution

Lemkin understood that throughout the history of the human race there have always been leaders who thought they could solve their problems not only through victory in war, but also by destroying entire national, ethnic, racial, or religious groups. Such annihilations of entire groups, in Lemkin's view, deprive the world of the very cultural diversity and richness in languages, traditions, values, and practices that distinguish the human race from all other life on earth. Genocide is not only unjust, it threatens the very existence and progress of human civilization, in Lemkin's eyes.

Looking to the past, Lemkin understood that the prevailing coarseness and brutality of earlier human societies and the lower value placed on human life obscured the existence of genocide. Sacrifice and exploitation, as well as torture and public execution, had been common at different times in history. Looking toward a more humane future, Lemkin asserted the need to punish—and when possible prevent—a crime for which there had been no name until he invented it.

Legal Definitions of Genocide

On December 9, 1948, the United Nations adopted its Convention on the Prevention and Punishment of the Crime of Genocide (UNGC). Under Article II, genocide:

> means any of the following acts committed with intent to destroy, in whole or in part, a national, ethnical, racial or religious group, as such:
>
> (a) Killing members of the group;
>
> (b) Causing serious bodily or mental harm to members of the group;
>
> (c) Deliberately inflicting on the group conditions of life calculated to bring about its physical destruction in whole or in part;
>
> (d) Imposing measures intended to prevent births within the group;
>
> (e) Forcibly transferring children of the group to another group.

Article III of the convention defines the elements of the crime of genocide, making punishable:

> (a) Genocide;
>
> (b) Conspiracy to commit genocide;
>
> (c) Direct and public incitement to commit genocide;
>
> (d) Attempt to commit genocide;
>
> (e) Complicity in genocide.

After intense debate, the architects of the convention excluded acts committed with intent to destroy social, political, and economic groups from the definition of genocide. Thus, attempts to destroy whole social classes—the physically and mentally challenged, and homosexuals, for example—are not acts of genocide under the terms of the UNGC. These groups achieved a belated but very significant measure of protection under international criminal law in the Rome Statute of the International Criminal

Court, adopted at a conference on July 17, 1998, and entered into force on July 1, 2002.

The Rome Statute defined a crime against humanity in the following way:

> any of the following acts when committed as part of a widespread and systematic attack directed against any civilian population:
>
> (a) Murder;
>
> (b) Extermination;
>
> (c) Enslavement;
>
> (d) Deportation or forcible transfer of population;
>
> (e) Imprisonment or other severe deprivation of physical liberty in violation of fundamental rules of international law;
>
> (f) Torture;
>
> (g) Rape, sexual slavery, enforced prostitution, forced pregnancy, enforced sterilization, or any other form of sexual violence of comparable gravity;
>
> (h) Persecution against any identifiable group or collectivity on political, racial, national, ethnic, cultural, religious, gender . . . or other grounds that are universally recognized as impermissible under international law, in connection with any act referred to in this paragraph or any crime within the jurisdiction of this Court;
>
> (i) Enforced disappearance of persons;
>
> (j) The crime of apartheid;
>
> (k) Other inhumane acts of a similar character intentionally causing great suffering, or serious injury to body or to mental or physical health.

Although genocide is often ranked as "the crime of crimes," in practice prosecutors find it much easier to convict perpetrators of crimes against humanity rather than genocide under domestic laws. However, while Article I of the UNGC declares that countries adhering to the UNGC recognize genocide as "a crime under international law which they undertake to prevent and to punish," the Rome Statute provides no comparable international mechanism for the prosecution of crimes against humanity. A treaty would help individual countries and international institutions introduce measures to prevent crimes against humanity, as well as open more avenues to the domestic and international prosecution of war criminals.

The Evolving Laws of Genocide

In the aftermath of the serious crimes committed against civilians in the former Yugoslavia since 1991 and the Rwanda genocide of 1994, the United Nations Security Council created special international courts to bring the alleged perpetrators of these events to justice. While the UNGC stands as the standard definition of genocide in law, the new courts contributed significantly to today's nuanced meaning of genocide, crimes against humanity, ethnic cleansing, and serious war crimes in international criminal law.

Also helping to shape contemporary interpretations of such mass atrocity crimes are the special and mixed courts for Sierra Leone, Cambodia, Lebanon, and Iraq, which may be the last of their type in light of the creation of the International Criminal Court (ICC), with its broad jurisdiction over mass atrocity crimes in all countries that adhere to the Rome Statute of the ICC. The Yugoslavia and Rwanda tribunals have already clarified the law of genocide, ruling that rape can be prosecuted as a weapon in committing genocide, evidence of intent can be absent when convicting low-level perpetrators of genocide, and public incitement to commit genocide is a crime even if genocide does not immediately follow the incitement.

Several current controversies about genocide are worth noting and will require more research in the future:

1. Dictators accused of committing genocide or persecution may hold onto power more tightly for fear of becoming

vulnerable to prosecution after they step down. Therefore, do threats of international indictments of these alleged perpetrators actually delay transfers of power to more representative rulers, thereby causing needless suffering?

2. Would the large sum of money spent for international retributive justice be better spent on projects directly benefiting the survivors of genocide and persecution?

3. Can international courts render justice impartially or do they deliver only "victors' justice," that is the application of one set of rules to judge the vanquished and a different and laxer set of rules to judge the victors?

It is important to recognize that the law of genocide is constantly evolving, and scholars searching for the roots and early warning signs of genocide may prefer to use their own definitions of genocide in their work. While the UNGC stands as the standard definition of genocide in law, the debate over its interpretation and application will never end. The ultimate measure of the value of any definition of genocide is its utility for identifying the roots of genocide and preventing future genocides.

Motives for Genocide and Early Warning Signs

When identifying past cases of genocide, many scholars work with some version of the typology of motives published in 1990 by historian Frank Chalk and sociologist Kurt Jonassohn in their book *The History and Sociology of Genocide*. The authors identify the following four motives and acknowledge that they may overlap, or several lesser motives might also drive a perpetrator:

1. To eliminate a real or potential threat, as in Imperial Rome's decision to annihilate Carthage in 146 BC.

2. To spread terror among real or potential enemies, as in Genghis Khan's destruction of city-states and people who rebelled against the Mongols in the thirteenth century.

3. To acquire economic wealth, as in the case of the Massachusetts Puritans' annihilation of the native Pequot people in 1637.

4. To implement a belief, theory, or an ideology, as in the case of Germany's decision under Hitler and the Nazis to destroy completely the Jewish people of Europe from 1941 to 1945.

Although these motives represent differing goals, they share common early warning signs of genocide. A good example of genocide in recent times that could have been prevented through close attention to early warning signs was the genocide of 1994 inflicted on the people labeled as "Tutsi" in Rwanda. Between 1959 and 1963, the predominantly Hutu political parties in power stigmatized all Tutsi as members of a hostile racial group, violently forcing their leaders and many civilians into exile in neighboring countries through a series of assassinations and massacres. Despite systematic exclusion of Tutsi from service in the military, government security agencies, and public service, as well as systematic discrimination against them in higher education, hundreds of thousands of Tutsi did remain behind in Rwanda. Government-issued cards identified each Rwandan as Hutu or Tutsi.

A generation later, some Tutsi raised in refugee camps in Uganda and elsewhere joined together, first organizing politically and then militarily, to reclaim a place in their homeland. When the predominantly Tutsi Rwanda Patriotic Front invaded Rwanda from Uganda in October 1990, extremist Hutu political parties demonized all of Rwanda's Tutsi as traitors, ratcheting up hate propaganda through radio broadcasts on government-run Radio Rwanda and privately owned radio station RTLM. Within the print media, *Kangura* and other publications used vicious cartoons to further demonize Tutsi and to stigmatize any Hutu who dared advocate bringing Tutsi into the government. Massacres of dozens and later hundreds of Tutsi sprang up even as Rwandans prepared to elect a coalition government led by moderate political parties, and as the United Nations dispatched a small international military force led by Canadian general Roméo Dallaire to oversee the elections and political transition. Late in 1992, an international human rights organization's investigating team detected the hate propaganda campaign, verified systematic massacres of Tutsi, and warned the international community that Rwanda had already entered the early stages of genocide, to no avail. On April 6, 1994, Rwanda's genocidal killing accelerated at an alarming pace when someone shot down the airplane flying Rwandan president Juvenal Habyarimana home from peace talks in Arusha, Tanzania.

Hundreds of thousands of Tutsi civilians—including children, women, and the elderly—died horrible deaths because the world ignored the early warning signs of the genocide and refused to act. Prominent among those early warning signs were: 1) systematic, government-decreed discrimination against the Tutsi as members of a supposed racial group; 2) government-issued identity cards labeling every Tutsi as a member of a racial group; 3) hate propaganda casting all Tutsi as subversives and traitors; 4) organized assassinations and massacres targeting Tutsi; and 5) indoctrination of militias and special military units to believe that all Tutsi posed a genocidal threat to the existence of Hutu and would enslave Hutu if they ever again became the rulers of Rwanda.

Genocide Prevention and the Responsibility to Protect

The shock waves emanating from the Rwanda genocide forced world leaders at least to acknowledge in principle that the national sovereignty of offending nations cannot trump the responsibility of those governments to prevent the infliction of mass atrocities on their own people. When governments violate that obligation, the member states of the United Nations have a responsibility to get involved. Such involvement can take the form of, first, offering to help the local government change its ways through technical advice and development aid, and second—if the local government persists in assaulting its own people—initiating armed intervention to protect the civilians at risk. In 2005 the United Nations began to implement the Responsibility to Protect initiative, a framework of principles to guide the international community in preventing mass atrocities.

As in many real-world domains, theory and practice often diverge. Genocide and crimes against humanity are rooted in problems that produce failing states: poverty, poor education, extreme nationalism, lawlessness, dictatorship, and corruption. Implementing the principles of the Responsibility to Protect doctrine burdens intervening state leaders with the necessity of addressing each of those problems over a long period of time. And when those problems prove too intractable and complex to solve easily, the citizens of the intervening nations may lose patience, voting out the leader who initiated the intervention. Arguments based solely on humanitarian principles fail to overcome such concerns. What is needed to persuade political leaders to stop preventable mass atrocities are compelling arguments based on their own national interests.

Preventable mass atrocities threaten the national interests of all states in five specific ways:

1. Mass atrocities create conditions that engender widespread and concrete threats from terrorism, piracy, and other forms of lawlessness on the land and sea;

2. Mass atrocities facilitate the spread of warlordism, whose tentacles block affordable access to vital raw materials produced in the affected country and threaten the prosperity of all nations that depend on the consumption of these resources;

3. Mass atrocities trigger cascades of refugees and internally displaced populations that, combined with climate change and growing international air travel, will accelerate the worldwide incidence of lethal infectious diseases;

4. Mass atrocities spawn single-interest parties and political agendas that drown out more diverse political discourse in the countries where the atrocities take place and in the countries that host large numbers of refugees. Xenophobia and nationalist backlashes are the predictable consequences of government indifference to mass atrocities elsewhere that could have been prevented through early actions;

5. Mass atrocities foster the spread of national and transnational criminal networks trafficking in drugs, women, arms, contraband, and laundered money.

Alerting elected political representatives to the consequences of mass atrocities should be part of every student movement's agenda in the twenty-first century. Adam Smith, the great political economist and author of *The Wealth of Nations*, put it best when he wrote: "It is not from the benevolence of the butcher, the brewer, or the baker that we expect our dinner, but from their regard to their own interest." Self-interest is a powerful engine for good in the marketplace and can be an equally powerful motive and source of inspiration for state action to prevent genocide and mass persecution. In today's new global village, the lives we save may be our own.

Frank Chalk

Frank Chalk, who has a doctorate from the University of Wisconsin-Madison, is a professor of history and director of the Montreal Institute for Genocide and Human Rights Studies at Concordia University in Montreal, Canada. He is coauthor, with Kurt

Jonassohn, of The History and Sociology of Genocide *(1990); coauthor with General Roméo Dallaire, Kyle Matthews, Carla Barqueiro, and Simon Doyle of* Mobilizing the Will to Intervene: Leadership to Prevent Mass Atrocities *(2010); and associate editor of the three-volume Macmillan Reference USA* Encyclopedia of Genocide and Crimes Against Humanity *(2004). Chalk served as president of the International Association of Genocide Scholars from June 1999 to June 2001. His current research focuses on the use of radio and television broadcasting in the incitement and prevention of genocide, and domestic laws on genocide. For more information on genocide and examples of the experiences of people displaced by genocide and other human rights violations, interested readers can consult the websites of the Montreal Institute for Genocide and Human Rights Studies (http://migs.concordia.ca) and the Montreal Life Stories project (www.lifestoriesmontreal.ca).*

World Map

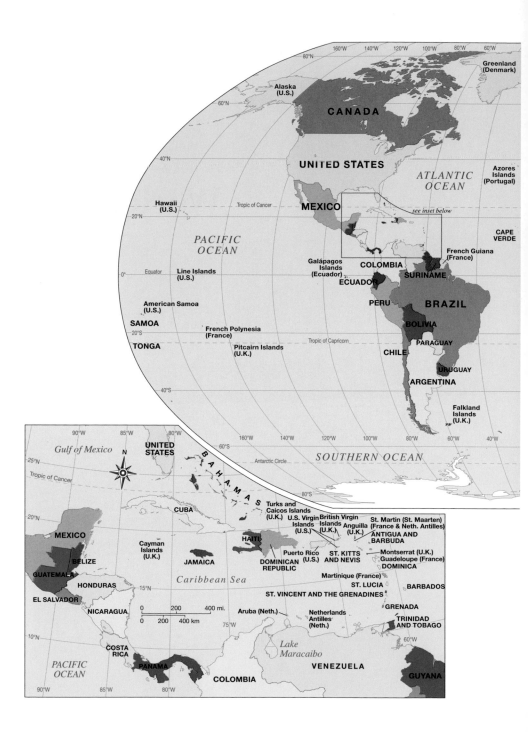

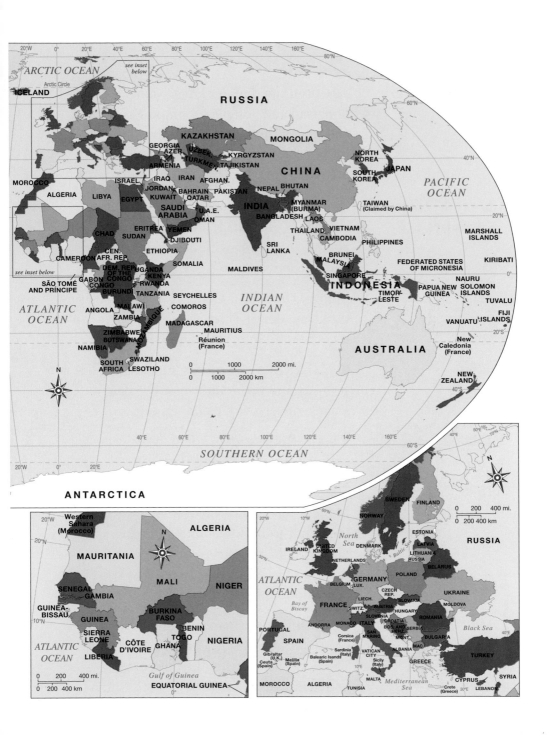

ARCTIC OCEAN

see inset below

Arctic Circle

ICELAND

RUSSIA

KAZAKHSTAN

MONGOLIA

GEORGIA
AZER.
ARMENIA
UZBEK.
TURKMEN.
KYRGYZSTAN
TAJIKISTAN

CHINA

NORTH
KOREA
SOUTH
KOREA

JAPAN

PACIFIC
OCEAN

MOROCCO

ALGERIA

LIBYA

ISRAEL
JORDAN
EGYPT
KUWAIT
IRAQ
BAHRAIN
QATAR
IRAN
AFGHAN.
PAKISTAN
NEPAL
BHUTAN

SAUDI
ARABIA
U.A.E.
OMAN
INDIA
MYANMAR
(BURMA)
BANGLADESH
LAOS

TAIWAN
(Claimed by China)

ERITREA
SUDAN
CHAD
YEMEN
DJIBOUTI
THAILAND
CAMBODIA
VIETNAM

SRI
LANKA

PHILIPPINES

MARSHALL
ISLANDS

CAMEROON
CEN.
AFR. REP.
ETHIOPIA
SOMALIA

MALDIVES

BRUNEI
MALAYSIA
SINGAPORE

FEDERATED STATES
OF MICRONESIA

KIRIBATI

GABON
SÃO TOMÉ
AND PRÍNCIPE
CONGO
DEM. REP.
OF THE
CONGO
UGANDA
KENYA
RWANDA
BURUNDI
TANZANIA
SEYCHELLES

INDIAN
OCEAN

INDONESIA

TIMOR-
LESTE

PAPUA NEW
GUINEA

NAURU
SOLOMON
ISLANDS

TUVALU

ATLANTIC
OCEAN

ANGOLA
MALAWI
ZAMBIA
COMOROS

MOZAMBIQUE

MADAGASCAR

MAURITIUS

Réunion
(France)

VANUATU
FIJI
ISLANDS

ZIMBABWE
BOTSWANA
NAMIBIA
SOUTH
AFRICA
SWAZILAND
LESOTHO

AUSTRALIA

New
Caledonia
(France)

NEW
ZEALAND

0   1000   2000 mi.
0   1000   2000 km

N

SOUTHERN OCEAN

ANTARCTICA

Western
Sahara
(Morocco)

ALGERIA

MAURITANIA

MALI

NIGER

N

SENEGAL
GAMBIA
GUINEA-
BISSAU
GUINEA
SIERRA
LEONE
LIBERIA

BURKINA
FASO
BENIN
TOGO
CÔTE
D'IVOIRE
GHANA

NIGERIA

ATLANTIC
OCEAN

Gulf of Guinea

EQUATORIAL GUINEA

0   200   400 mi.
0   200 400 km

NORWAY
SWEDEN
FINLAND

ESTONIA

IRELAND
UNITED
KINGDOM
North
Sea
DENMARK
Baltic Sea
LATVIA
LITHUANIA
RUSSIA

RUSSIA

NETHERLANDS
GERMANY
POLAND
BELARUS

ATLANTIC
OCEAN

Bay of
Biscay
BELGIUM
LUX.
LIECH.
CZECH
REP.
SLOVAKIA
UKRAINE
MOLDOVA

FRANCE
SWITZ.
AUSTRIA
HUNGARY
SLOVENIA
ROMANIA

ANDORRA
MONACO
ITALY
SAN
MARINO
CROATIA
BOS. AND
HERZ.
SERBIA
MONT.
BULGARIA

Black Sea

PORTUGAL
SPAIN
Corsica
(France)
Sardinia
(Italy)
VATICAN
CITY
ALBANIA
MAC.

GREECE

TURKEY

Gibraltar
(U.K.)
Ceuta
(Spain)
Melilla
(Spain)
Balearic Isands
(Spain)
Sicily
(Italy)
MALTA
Mediterranean
Sea
CYPRUS
SYRIA
LEBANON

MOROCCO

ALGERIA

TUNISIA

Crete
(Greece)

0   200   400 mi.
0   200 400 km

Chronology

Seventh Century	Tibet is unified under kings Namri Songtsan and Songtsan Gampo. Songtsan Gampo also introduces Buddhism to Tibet and establishes contact with China's Tang Dynasty.
Seventh–Thirteenth Centuries	Tibet's influence grows due to its location along the "Silk Road," the trade routes connecting China with the Middle East and Europe.
1207	Mongol conqueror Genghis Khan forces the surrender of Tibet, which is soon incorporated into Yuan Dynasty China.
1290	Kublai Khan, emperor of China's Yuan Dynasty and the grandson of Genghis Khan, converts to Tibetan Buddhism.
1368	Tibet becomes independent once again with the fall of the Yuan Dynasty.
1578	The title of Dalai Lama is established by Mongol ruler Altan Khan when he grants the honor to Buddhist monk Sonam Gyatso. Sonam Gyatso is recognized as the third Dalai Lama, with the first two being honored posthumously.
1617–1682	The fifth Dalai Lama, Ngawang Lozang Gyatso, is born. As leader, he extends Tibet's borders to their furthest extent and maintains relations with both China and India.

1740   Polhawa, head of one of the quarrel-
ing factions then trying to rule Tibet,
is named king by officials representing
China's Q'ing Dynasty. This supports
China's later claim that Tibet is part of
greater China.

1903   A force of British soldiers under the
command of Francis Younghusband
invades Tibet, seeking to force a connection between Tibet and British-held
India. The current Dalai Lama, the thirteenth, escapes to China.

1909   The thirteenth Dalai Lama returns to
Tibet, now seeking British help against
growing Chinese interference in Tibet.

1911   Chinese leader Yuan Shikai, takes power
after the fall of the Q'ing Dyasty, China's
last traditional dynastic regime. He declares Tibet to be a Chinese province.

1912   Tibetan troops defeat a Chinese force
and require a formal surrender.

1913   The thirteenth Dalai Lama declares Tibet
to be independent. The British grant
recognition to Tibet but China refuses to
do so.

1935   The fourteenth Dalai Lama, Tenzin
Gyatso, is born. He receives his formal
title in 1940.

1949   The Communist Party of China under
Mao Zedong succeeds in its long struggle
to take over China. Mao pledges to use

	his People's Liberation Army (PLA) to "liberate" Tibet and bring it under Chinese control.
1950	The PLA enters the long-disputed territory of central Tibet.
1951	Tibet and China enter into a 17-Point Agreement that establishes Tibet as one of China's "National Autonomous Regions." Tibet loses its independence but is still promised a large degree of self-government. The Dalai Lama and other leaders ratify the agreement.
1954	Tibetans begin revolting against Chinese authority when Chinese troops and officials initiate the destruction of monasteries as well as economic and social reforms.
1956	The Dalai Lama first seeks exile in India but returns to Tibet when Chinese leaders promise no further drastic reforms.
1958–1962	China's so-called Great Leap Forward, a massive attempt at state-directed economic development, ensues. Many Tibetans become forced laborers or are imprisoned.
March 10, 1959	Large-scale protests begin in Lhasa, Tibet's capital.
March 17, 1959	The Dalai Lama goes into exile in India, to be followed by tens of thousands of other Tibetans. His new base becomes Dharamsala in northern India.

March 19, 1959	Widespread outbreaks of violence begin when Tibetan soldiers join the protests against Chinese authority.
March 23, 1959	PLA troops end the rebellion. Soon after, China steps up its destruction of monasteries and many Tibetans are placed in forced-labor camps.
1966	China's Great Proletarian Cultural Revolution begins. As part of this attempt to overturn centuries of tradition, many of the remaining Tibetan monasteries are destroyed and other features of Tibetan culture and life are strongly suppressed.
1976	The Cultural Revolution ends with the death of Mao Zedong.
1979	China's new leader, Deng Xiaoping, tries to soften relations with Tibet by inviting the Dalai Lama to return on the condition that he remain in Beijing. The Dalai Lama refuses but sends a fact-finding mission to Tibet.
1980–1987	The Dalai Lama tries, without much success, to start positive negotiations with Chinese leaders. His overall goal is autonomy, or self-government, rather than complete independence for Tibet.
1987	A new series of pro-autonomy demonstrations in Lhasa begins.
1988	The Dalai Lama makes the so-called Strasbourg Proposal, in which China

	would retain control of Tibet's foreign policy and military defense but would otherwise leave Tibet independent. China pledges to consider the proposal.
March 5, 1989	Demonstrations in Lhasa result in widespread arrests and dozens of alleged killings, as well as a declaration of martial law by the PLA. Foreign tourists and journalists are forced to leave.
October 5, 1989	The Dalai Lama is awarded the Nobel Peace Prize.
1990–1991	The Tibetan Parliament in Exile, part of the Central Tibetan Administration in Dharamsala, India, begins to take shape.
1995	Controversy arises when the Dalai Lama names a six-year-old boy the Panchen Lama. Chinese authorities place the child under house arrest and back another candidate as Panchen Lama.
2006	The rail link between Tibet's capital, Lhasa, and the Chinese capital of Beijing is completed. Some Tibetans fear it will enable greater economic and cultural interference.
March 2008	The Summer Olympic Games, to be held that summer in Beijing, inspire anti-Chinese demonstrations by Tibetans and other minorities.
October 2008	The Dalai Lama claims that he has lost hope that China and Tibet can ever reach an agreement.

2009	Ahead of what it fears will be demonstrations and other protests marking the 50th anniversary of the 1959 uprising, China detains many alleged "criminals" and closes Tibet to tourists for two months. China also names its candidate for Panchen Lama as China's official spokesman for Tibet.
March 2011	Tibetan monks and other activists begin a series of self-immolations as acts of protest. These continue into 2012 and 2013.
November 2011	The Dalai Lama formally hands over his political responsibilities to the speaker of the Tibetan Parliament in Exile.

Historical Background on Tibet

Chapter Exercises

STATISTICS	
	Tibet Autonomous Region*
Total Area	1,228,400 sq km (474,300 sq mi) World ranking: 55 (if listed as a separate nation)
Population	3,002,166 World ranking: 138 (if listed as a separate nation)
Ethnic Groups	Tibetan 92.8%,, Han Chinese 6.1%, Monpa 0.3%, Hui 0.3%, other 0.2%
Religions	Tibetan Buddhism about 89%, Bon about 10%, Islam (<1%), Christianity (<1%)
Literacy (total population)	37.8% (Tibet Autonomous Region) 92.2% (China)
GDP	$9.6 billion (Tibet Autonomous Region) $12.38 trillion (China) World ranking: 132 (if listed as a separate nation)

* Tibet is not an independent nation but part of the People's Republic of China. Statistics are for what China calls the Tibet Autonomous Region.

Source: *The World Factbook*. Washington, DC: Central Intelligence Agency, 2013. www.cia.gov.

1. Analyze the Table

Question 1: The vast majority of people in the Tibet Autonomous Region are ethnic Tibetans, but the largest minority group consists of Han Chinese (the dominant ethnic group in China as a whole). How might this minority have aided in China's absorption of Tibet, and how might it be argued that Han Chinese are "displacing" the Tibetans, especially in positions of power and influence?

Question 2: Tibet's literacy rate is low compared to China's as a whole. What factors might help explain the difference?

Question 3: The great majority of Tibetans follow their own distinct version of Buddhism, while China is an officially atheist state whose Communist ideology rejects religions. Would you argue that Tibetan Buddhism is an important source of the conflict between Tibet and China?

2. Writing Prompt

Write an article that describes the Chinese crackdown in Tibet in 1959 and the subsequent exile of the Dalai Lama and other Tibetan leaders. Include a strong title that will capture the reader's attention. Be sure to provide the necessary background information as well as important names, places, and ideas.

3. Group Activity

Form small groups and examine how recent events such as the completion of the Beijing-Lhasa railway and the 2008 Summer Olympics in Beijing affected relations between China and Tibet. Write a policy statement suggesting how the United Nations or other international organizations might respond to these incidents.

A Brief History of Tibet

Alex McKay

In the following viewpoint, Alex McKay provides a brief history of Tibet. He describes how over the centuries this dry isolated region has known periods as a military power, a state seeking protection from powerful neighbors such as the Chinese or Mongols, and even a target of British imperialists. McKay also notes the centrality of the Buddhist religion in Tibet's culture and how its population now includes large numbers of recently-arrived ethnic Chinese, or Han. McKay's books on Tibet include Tibet and Her Neighbors *and* Pilgrimage in Tibet.

Traditionally, Tibet comprises the central Asian landmass between the Himalayas in the south, the Kunlun range to the north and the Karakorams to the west, while in the east it is bounded by the region of the great rivers, the Chang (Yangtze), Mekong, and Salween. With most of its territory situated above 4,500 meters [14,763 feet] and its capital city, Lhasa, located at 3,607 meters [11,834 feet], Tibet has been popularly termed "The Roof of the World."

While the extent to which Tibet was part of China in earlier periods is in dispute, Tibet has certainly been part of China since

Alex McKay, "Tibet," *Encyclopedia of Modern Asia*, vol. 5, edited by Karen Christensen, 2003, pp. 484–486. Copyright © 2003 by Cengage Learning. Reproduced by permission.

the Communist invasion in 1950, and exists today only in the much-reduced area of the Tibetan Autonomous Region (TAR) of China. A Tibetan Government-in-exile headed by the Dalai Lama (the spiritual and temporal leader of the Tibetan peoples), has been established in India, and there are also Tibetan exile communities in Switzerland and the United States. The Tibetan government continues to campaign for Tibetan self-determination and the ongoing Sino-Tibetan dispute invests facts and figures in regard to Tibet with important political implications. Historically, however, there has been a distinction between "political" Tibet, the area ruled by the Lhasa government prior to 1950, and "ethnic" or "cultural" Tibet, that area inhabited by mainly Buddhist peoples of Tibetan origin.

Geography and History

"Political" Tibet had an estimated population of between 1.8 and 3 million peoples, of whom around half were semi-nomadic yak herders. (Today's TAR population includes a large number of Han Chinese immigrants, who may now constitute a majority of the population in the Tibetan capital of Lhasa.) The settled urban and agricultural populations were concentrated in the river valleys, particularly in the triangle formed by the major settlements of Lhasa, Shigatse (Xigaze) and Gyantse.

While situated at a latitude similar to Algeria, the altitude and location of the Tibetan plateau produces a cold and generally dry climate, although southeastern Tibet includes areas of tropical jungle. The western Tibetan area around the Gangdise (Kailas) mountain range and Lake Mapam Yumco (Manasarowar) is the source of four great rivers: the Indus, Ganges, Brahmaputra, and the Sutlej, while Mount Everest, which is situated on the Nepal-Tibet border, is, at 8,848 meters [29,029 feet] the world's highest mountain.

Sedentary agriculture is limited by the climate. Barley is the major crop and in its roasted form as *tsampa* comprises, with yak meat and tea (imported from China), the staple diet of the majority of the population.

The Potala Palace in Tibet's capital, Lhasa, is the former home of the fourteenth Dalai Lama, Tibet's political and spiritual leader, who was exiled to India in 1959. © Gonzalo Azumendi/ age fotostock/Getty Images.

The origins of the Tibetan peoples appear to be linked to Central Asian nomadic tribes such as the Qiang and Yue Zhi (Tokharians). The first unified Tibetan state was a tribal confederacy formed in the seventh century under the rule of King Songtsen Gampo (or Srong-brtsan Sgam-po; c. 608–650 CE), who established his capital at Lhasa. The introduction of a Tibetan script and Buddhist teachings are among the innovations attributed to his reign. The dynasty he founded lasted until the assassination of King Langdharma, around the year 842.

Tibet was a formidable military power during this period, constantly engaged in warfare with neighboring powers and strong enough to sack the Chinese capital of Xi'an in 763. At its height the Tibetan empire reached as far west as Samarqand. Buddhism became increasingly important, particularly in the court, and the first Tibetan monastery was established at Samye around 779. But there was considerable opposition to the new faith among aristocratic factions associated with followers of the indigenous Tibetan belief system (later identified with the Bon faith but probably at that time an unsystematized tradition that included elements of divine kingship and sacrificial practice).

Buddhism became firmly established during the eleventh and twelfth centuries, when Indian Buddhist texts were systematically translated into the Tibetan language. Of the four major sects of Tibetan Buddhism that developed on the basis of these teachings, the Gelugpa sect eventually emerged as preeminent, and from the sixteenth century onwards, Tibet was ruled by a line of incarnate Gelugpa monks with the title of dalai lama. Religious factions in Tibet tended to seek Mongol or Chinese patronage, and China became increasingly involved in events in Tibet in the eighteenth century. Thus, from 1793 until 1911–1912, China was able to exert at least nominal suzerainty over Lhasa.

In 1903–1904, the British imperial Government of India dispatched a mission to Lhasa that forced the Tibetans to accept British representatives and effectively opened the country to Western ideas and influences. But despite some modernization in the next couple of decades, Tibet remained an essentially conservative religious society, strongly resistant to change. The thirteenth Dalai Lama (1876–1933), a strong nationalist leader, led Tibet to independence after the Chinese revolution in 1911, and Tibet survived as a de facto independent state until the Communist Chinese invasion in 1950. Her independence, however, was not officially recognized by any major powers, with China continuing to claim Tibet as part of her territory.

Since 1950, the Tibetans have suffered a continuous assault on their cultural identity, with tens or even hundreds of thousands of Tibetans killed, imprisoned, and tortured as a result of Chinese colonialist policies.

A Culture Largely Shaped by Buddhism

Despite the continuing existence of the Bon faith and its many cultural manifestations, the outstanding feature of Tibetan culture is generally considered to be its unique form of Buddhism, a synthesis of the Mahayana and Tantric forms of the faith. Buddhist influence permeated virtually all aspects of traditional society. An estimated 20 percent of the male population were monks, and more than six thousand monasteries were distributed throughout the Tibetan cultural world. These were important political and economic centers as well as the guardians of Tibetan cultural and artistic expression. Outside of the monasteries, pilgrimage to sacred cities and mountains was a particularly significant religious expression for all classes of people.

A small aristocratic class enjoyed considerable privilege, although in comparison to their contemporaries in neighboring states, the Tibetan peasantry were tolerably well treated. Women too, enjoyed greater than average freedom, particularly in the social and economic spheres, although they were almost entirely excluded from religious power.

There were cultural influences from both China and India, but Tibetan culture was strikingly distinct from that of its neighbors. This was particularly marked in such areas as literary traditions (in particular the lengthy *Gesar of Ling* epic), language, and art and architecture, with buildings such as Lhasa's Potala Palace and Jokhang temple, as well as the regional monasteries, being of striking originality. Much of this culture has been destroyed in the TAR, but much has been remembered or preserved in exile.

Tibet Has a Long and Complex History with China

Encyclopedia of Modern China

China's major claim to legitimate control over Tibet is that the region has always been a part of China, or at least part of China's larger sphere of influence. The following viewpoint from the Encyclopedia of Modern China *explores that claim. It describes how during the Qing Dynasty (1644–1912), the last of several imperial dynasties that ruled China for thousands of years, the two regions developed a close relationship. This bond was based partly on the threat of a common enemy, the nomadic Mongols, and involved the continued presence of Qing imperial officials in Lhasa, Tibet's capital. Yet the viewpoint also indicates that, as the Qing Dynasty weakened in the 1800s, so did its hold over Tibet. By the early 1900s Tibetan leaders, notably the Dalai Lama, were ready to pursue national independence rather than status as a recognized "nationality" under Chinese authority. But in 1951, Tibet came under Communist Chinese rule officially, and tensions and hostilities continued.*

The current debate over Tibet's political status and its relations with China has deep roots going back to the empire building of the Qing dynasty (1644–1912). When the Qing forces penetrated Qinghai in the mid-1640s, an alliance between the Qing and the Tibetans was in the interest of both parties. The Tibetans wished to establish a friendly relationship with the new dominant power in China and Inner Asia, and the Qing court sought to use Tibetan Buddhism to strengthen its ties with the Mongols. The visit of the Fifth Dalai Lama (1617–1682) to Beijing in 1653 demonstrates this unusual relationship between the early Qing and the Tibetans.

With the consolidation of Qing control in China, and the decline of Mongol power in Inner Asia, the Qing was able to intervene in Tibet without regard for Tibet's role in Inner Asian affairs. From 1720 to the late eighteenth century, the Qing gradually increased its authority in Tibet, intervening in the case of third-party invasions of Tibet (1720 and 1792) and internal disorders (1728 and 1750). Each intervention resulted in an increase in Qing administrative control over Tibetan affairs. Two permanent *ambans*, Qing imperial residents, were installed in Lhasa in 1727 to closely superintend Tibetan affairs. This arrangement was reinforced by the presence of a Qing garrison force in Tibet, which indicated the strengthened Qing military authority there.

In 1792, after successfully repelling the invading Gurkhas in Tibet, the Qing court took the occasion to extensively restructure its protectorate over Tibet. The status of the *ambans* was elevated above that of the Dalai Lama. They not only took control of Tibetan defense and foreign affairs, but were also put in command of the Qing garrison and the Tibetan army. The Qing also required that the incarnations of the Dalai and Panchen Lamas be chosen with the supervision of the *ambans*. This meant that the final authority over the selection of reincarnations, and thus over political succession in the Tibetan system of combined spiritual and temporal rule, would henceforth belong to the Qing government.

The Decline of Qing Power in Tibet

The measure put into effect in 1792 represented the height of Qing influence in Tibet. Thereafter, the Qing became increasingly preoccupied with problems in the interior, and officials in Beijing found it less and less easy to intervene in Tibetan affairs. When the Gurkhas [from Nepal] again attacked Tibet in 1855, the Qing was so preoccupied with the Taiping Uprising (1851–1864) that it was unable to respond to the Tibetans' request for assistance. Thus, the Tibetans were forced to pay tribute to Nepal and grant judicial extraterritoriality to Nepalese subjects in Tibet. By the second half of the nineteenth century, the Qing *ambans*, who represented the Qing emperor and Qing authority, could do little more than exercise ritualistic and symbolic influence.

In 1895 Qing China suffered defeat in the war with Japan, thus beginning the final decline of the dynastic order. The final years of the dynasty witnessed the rise of Han Chinese nationalism, in reaction to both foreign imperialism and the alien rule of the Manchus. Meanwhile, competition between the British and Russian empires over influence in Central Asia began to transform Tibet into an object of international interest. In order to ward off possible threats from the north and thus protect its position in India, the British regarded it essential to maintain a sphere of influence and a military buffer in Tibet. In 1904, in order to counteract growing Russian activity in Tibet, the British launched a military expedition to the region. As a result of this invasion, the British secured certain trade privileges and were allowed to open three trade marts at Gyantse, Yatung, and Gartok. In subsequent treaties, the British further secured the guarantee that Qing China would exclude all other foreign powers from Tibet, thus preventing Russian interference in Tibet. In terms of the concept of international law, these treaties signed between Britain and Qing China also affirmed Qing overlordship in that region.

Late Qing Reforms in Tibet

The British invasion of Tibet in 1904 had far-reaching implications in terms of contemporary Tibetan issues. It ended Tibet's century-long international isolation. It also established direct relations between the British and the Tibetans, upon which Tibet might theoretically have built a case for international recognition as an independent state. Meanwhile, the growth of British interest and activity in Tibet caused Qing China to attempt to restore its precarious position in Lhasa. In 1905 the Qing initiated a series of new programs to consolidate central authority in southwest China. These programs included eliminating local autonomous Tibetan chiefdoms in the Kham (Eastern Tibet) area, and reducing the number of monks in monasteries.

Beijing's new deals caused wide disaffection locally, and in one uprising a Qing *amban* was killed. In swift retaliation, the Qing sent an army to suppress the rebellion and reinforce its authority over Tibet. The Qing reforms shocked the Thirteenth Dalai Lama (1876–1933). Frustrated that the Qing troops were sent to Tibet to ensure China's control over him, in 1910 the Dalai Lama decided to flee into exile in India. Beijing responded by deposing him. However, the Qing in the 1900s was by no means comparable to the Qing in the 1700s. With the outbreak of the Chinese revolution in 1911, the Qing's proactive policies over Tibet became unsustainable. Taking advantage of the chaotic situation in China proper, the Tibetans demanded the withdrawal of all Chinese soldiers and officials from Tibet. Chinese troops were finally removed from Tibet in late 1912.

Republican China and Tibet

With the ousting of Qing troops, along with Chinese authority, from Tibet, the status of Tibet as part of China's frontier territory became a highly controversial issue that would remain unresolved throughout the subsequent Republican era (1912–1949). Immediately after its foundation on January 1, 1912, the Chinese Republic began to show interest in transforming the Inner Asian dependencies of the defunct Qing into integral parts of the Chinese state. Yuan Shikai, president of the new Republic, propagated a doctrine of equality among the "five nationalities" of China—the Han, Manchu, Mongols, Tibetans, and Hui

Muslims—the major component peoples of the former Qing empire. This five-nationality doctrine was premised upon the Han Chinese belief that border peoples only wanted equal treatment under a Chinese administration, not freedom from Chinese control altogether. However, the Dalai Lama, who in 1912 returned to Lhasa with British patronage, was no longer prepared to accept Chinese authority over his territory.

In 1913 and 1914, the British proposed that a tripartite conference on Tibet's status be held at Simla, India, and Beijing was forced to accept the participation of Tibetan delegates at this event on an equal footing. No consensus concerning Tibet's status was reached at the conference. The Tibetans claimed independence from Chinese authority, whereas the Chinese uncompromisingly insisted on maintaining China's sovereignty over Tibet. China's verbal sovereignty over Tibet continued after the Nationalists under Chiang Kai-shek (Jiang Jieshi) came to power in 1928. Throughout the Republican period, against a backcloth of British patronage, a relatively weak Chinese central regime, and a chaotic situation in China proper, the Tibetans enjoyed an independent status free from Chinese dominance, even if such independence was *de facto*, not *de jure* [in fact, not in law].

Tibet Under Communist Chinese Rule

After defeating Nationalist forces in the Chinese civil war (1946–1949), the Communist People's Liberation Army (PLA) invaded Qamdo, crushing the ill-equipped Tibetan army, which offered little resistance. In May 1951, Tibetan representatives in Beijing were forced to sign a Seventeen-point Agreement with the Communist leadership. The accord acknowledged China's sovereignty over Tibet. A few months later, the Fourteenth Dalai Lama ratified the agreement.

At the initial stage of Communist rule, the Dalai Lama was assured that his status, along with Tibet's traditional dual political-religious system, would remain intact. However, Beijing's ultimate goal was to integrate Tibet into China through

Chinese administration and other reforms. In March 1955, the preparatory committee to rule the TAR [Tibet Autonomous Region] was first established. Meanwhile, land redistribution and "democratic" reforms were introduced outside the political boundary of the TAR in the ethnic Tibetan areas of Qinghai, Yunnan, and Kham, which caused local revolts to erupt. By late 1958, the PLA was instructed to pacify the revolts in Kham and Qinghai. Local Tibetans began moving into the TAR, toward Lhasa. In Lhasa, tensions also reached a critical point by the middle of 1958. The Chinese Communists accused the Dalai Lama and his government of sympathizing with anti-Chinese resisters and of supplying them with arms. The tensions finally reached a climax in March 1959. No longer able to control the situation in Tibet, the Dalai Lama fled from Lhasa to India with U.S. covert aid. In 1960 the Indian government permitted the Dalai Lama and his followers to establish a "government-in-exile" in Dharamsala, which continues today.

By May 1959, the Tibetan revolt was over. The absence of the Dalai Lama facilitated Chinese Communist control over Tibet. Beijing abolished the Dalai Lama's administration system and replaced it with Communist control. Tibet was reorganized into more than seventy rural counties and special districts to replace the feudal governing structure. In urban areas, street and local committees were established to manage local security, hold public meetings, and regulate population movement. In rural areas, Communist-dominated peasant associations also regulated local affairs. Although these administrative changes helped Beijing control Tibetan society, tensions and conflicts between the Han Chinese and the Tibetans continued. In March 1989, tension in Lhasa reached a new height, forcing the Chinese to impose martial law over the next twelve months.

China-Tibetan Tangles

Since 1959, the self-exiled Tibetan government in Dharamsala has attracted thousands of Tibetan refugees to join its Free Tibet movement. Yet the Dalai Lama's exiled leadership could not agree on goals. On the one hand, the Dalai Lama extolled the virtues of being ready to return to Tibet. On the other hand, in order for refugees to raise themselves above bare subsistence, it is essential that the government-in-exile deepen its social foundation in its governed communities and interact more closely with its Indian neighbors. For several decades after 1959, the Dalai Lama and his advisers were unable to reconcile these goals.

Beginning in the late 1970s, the Chinese government initiated a dialogue with the Dalai Lama to have him return to China and achieve the final legitimation of Chinese rule in Tibet. The Dalai Lama responded in his 1988 Strasbourg address by formally accepting Chinese sovereignty over Tibet in exchange for genuine and well-defined autonomous rights for Tibetans. By proposing Tibetan autonomy, the Dalai Lama implied a Tibet governed by the Tibetans themselves under China's legal and territorial framework, rather than seeking Tibet's political independence from Chinese jurisdiction. Yet his proposal was ignored by the Chinese to whom it was directed, and by Tibetans who rejected it. His proposal only impressed the international community, for whom the fundamental issues of sovereignty and independence were not as important as the Dalai Lama's spirit of concession toward resolving an international conflict.

In the 1990s, Beijing was little disposed to compromise on Tibet, because a solution to that problem seemed finally within its grasp. Beijing was convinced that any autonomy, cultural or political, would only revive Tibetan nationalism and encourage Tibetan demands for greater autonomy, including independence. After the riots of 1987 to 1989, Beijing formulated a new strategy to resolve the Tibet issue. It offered a program of colonization under the guise of Tibet's separate development. This strategy was accompanied by continuous education and ideological indoctrination to win over Tibetans. Beijing's 1994 decision to revive its long-delayed plan to complete a railroad link via Golmud to Lhasa also demonstrates a policy of colonial flexibility that uses both traditional Chinese frontier policy and an admission that the Communist promise of national minority autonomy was only meant to achieve assimilation. The building of the new railroad, which is part of the Great Western Development Scheme launched in 2000, has generated a hostile response from Tibetans, both in the TAR and in exile, who perceive it as a potential threat of further Han dominance, politically, religiously, and culturally. Whether China's policy will effectively settle its Tibet issue and Beijing's relations with the Dalai Lama remains to be seen.

The Seventeen-Point Agreement Between China and Tibet

Government of China

In 1949 Mao Zedong's Communist Party of China took the nation's capital, Beijing, and inaugurated a new regime: the People's Republic of China. In 1951, after the People's Liberation Army entered Tibet, the new government signed an agreement with Tibetan leaders summarized in the following viewpoint. Its seventeen points require Tibetan leaders to assist the Chinese in incorporating the region into the new communist China. The agreement also suggests that Tibetans will enjoy a degree of regional and cultural autonomy, or freedom. Chinese leaders assumed, as many Tibetans did not, that Tibet had always been a part of China rather than an independent state. In later years this seventeen-point agreement provided reasons for both China's continued incursions into Tibet as well as resistance by Tibetan rebels.

17 Point Agreement 23rd May 1951.

1. The Tibetan people shall unite and drive out imperialist aggressive force from Tibet; the Tibetan people shall

"17 Point Agreements," as found on Friends of Tibet (NZ), May 23, 1951. Reproduced by permission.

return to the big family of the Motherland—the People's Republic of China.

2. The local government of Tibet shall actively assist the PLA [China's People's Liberation Army] to enter Tibet and consolidate the national defences.

3. In accordance with the policy towards nationalities laid down in the Common Programme of the CPPCC [Chinese People's Political Consultative Conference, a governmental body], the Tibetan people have the right of exercising national regional autonomy under the unified leadership of the CPG [Chinese People's Government].

4. The central authorities will not alter the existing political system in Tibet. The central authorities also will not alter the established status, functions and the power of the Dalai Lama. Officials of various ranks shall hold office as usual.

5. The established status, functions and powers of the Panchen Ngerhtehni shall be maintained.

6. By the established status, functions and powers of the Dalai Lama and of the Panchen Ngoerhtehni are meant the status, functions and powers of the thirteenth Dalai Lama and of the Panchen Ngoerhtehni when they were friendly and amicable relations with each other.

7. The policy of freedom of religious belief laid down in the Common Programme of the CPCC shall be carried out. The religious beliefs, customs and habits of the Tibetan people shall be respected and lama monasteries shall be protected. The central authorities will not effect a change in the income of the monasteries.

8. Tibetan troops shall be reorganised step by step into the PLA and become a part of the national defence force of the CPR [Chinese People's Republic].

9. The spoken and written language and school education of

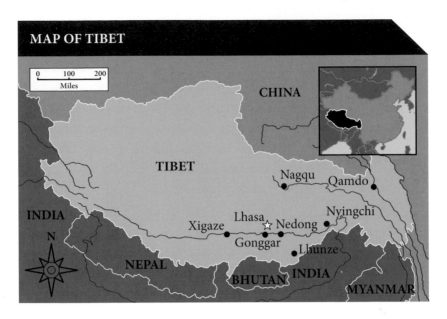

MAP OF TIBET

the Tibetan nationality shall be developed step by step in accordance with the actual condition in Tibet.

10. Tibetan agriculture, livestock raising, industry and commerce shall be developed step by step and the people's livelihood shall be improved step by step in accordance with the actual condition in Tibet.

11. In matters related to various reforms in Tibet, there will be no compulsion on the part of the central authorities. The local government of Tibet should carry out reforms of its own accord, and when the people raise demands for reform; they shall be settled by means of consultation with the leading personnel of Tibet.

12. In so far as former pro-Kuomintang officials [enemies of Communist China during the 1945–49 civil war] resolutely sever relations with imperialist and the Kuomintang and do not engage in sabotage or resistance, they may continue to hold office irrespective of their past.

13. The PLA entering Tibet shall abide by all the above-

mentioned policies and shall also be fair in all buying and selling and shall not arbitrarily take a needle or thread from the people.

14. The CPG shall have centralised handling of all external affairs of the area of Tibet; and there will be peaceful Co-existence with neighbouring countries and establishment and development of fair commercial and trading relations with them on basis of equality, mutual benefit and mutual respect for territory and sovereignty.

15. In order to ensure the implementation of this agreement, the CPG shall set up a Military and Administrative Committee and a Military Area HQ [headquarters] in Tibet. And—apart from the personnel sent there by the CPG—shall absorb as many local Tibetan personnel as possible to take part in the work. Local Tibetan personnel taking part in the Military and Administrative Committee may include patriotic elements from the local government of Tibet, various districts and various principle monasteries; the name-list shall be set forth after consultation between the representatives designed by the CPG and various quarters concerned and shall be submitted to the CPG for appointment.

16. Funds needed by the Military and Administrative Committee, the Military Area HQ and the PLA entering Tibet shall be provided by the CPG. The local government of Tibet should assist the PLA in the purchase and transport of food, fodder and other daily necessities.

17. This agreement shall come into force immediately after signature and seal are fixed on it.

Tibet Uprising and Resistance

James Steinberg

Although Communist China first began to assert its control over Tibet in 1950, the decisive moment in modern relations between the two peoples came in 1959. In the following viewpoint, scholar and diplomat James Steinberg describes the key events of that year. By 1959 many of Tibet's key tribal factions and groups of leaders, notably those in monasteries, had grown suspicious of China's heavy-handed attempts to impose centralized authority from Beijing, China's capital. After years of smaller outbreaks of violence in outlying areas, a major rebellion arose in 1959 in Tibet's capital, Lhasa. One result, Steinberg writes, was the killing of some 80,000 Tibetans by China's People's Liberation Army (PLA). Another was the exile of the Dalai Lama, Tibet's spiritual and political leader, to Dharamsala in India, although Steinberg notes that his departure had little impact on China's overall strategy. Steinberg is a dean and professor of social science, international affairs, and law at Syracuse University. He has also served as Deputy United States Secretary of State.

In 1959 a major rebellion erupted in Lhasa, the capital of Tibet, as thousands of Tibetans gathered to protect their threatened

James Steinberg, "Tibet Uprising and Resistance," *The International Encyclopedia of Revolution and Protest: 1500 to the Present*, edited by Immanuel Ness, 7th ed., 2009, pp. 3290–3293. Reproduced by permission.

religious leader, the fourteenth Dalai Lama. The uprising culminated after ten years of intrusive Chinese military and political coercion that turned more violent by early 1952. The new Chinese communist regime began in 1949, led by Mao Zedong (1893–1976), who began a subtle and intentional strategy to spread the communist revolution to Tibet and lay claim to the region as an integral part of China. As the Chinese began to move into the region in the 1950s, tensions increased between the Chinese communists and the Tibetans (who are by and large devout Yellow Hat Buddhists, a local sect founded in the fifteenth century).

In 1950, the Chinese People's Liberation Army (PLA) defeated the Tibetan army at Chamdo (in outer Tibet); however, they ceased their offensive and sent an ultimatum to the Dalai Lama. The Chinese strategy was to force the Tibetans into negotiating a settlement and allow the Chinese to move into the region, building roads and electrical stations. Using agreements and committees, they sought to reassure the Tibetans that changes would not be immediate, and Lhasa (in central Tibet) would be left alone for six years. The communists' aim was the "peaceful liberation" of Tibet, and their strategy was to show a united front to reduce resistance by the Tibetan people and convince Tibet to accept the changes.

In 1952, Chinese officials began imposing a socialist transformation on Tibetans living in outlying areas of the capital. The Chinese engaged in dismantling religion as monks were imprisoned and chased from monasteries. The hostilities by the Chinese led to rebellions in these areas as Tibetan Khampa and Ambowas were outraged by the abuse and murder of their own people. As tribal Tibetans continued to rebel and the casualties mounted, the Chinese, however, did not engage in hostilities in Lhasa, the residence of their god-king, the Dalai Lama. The Chinese created intolerable conditions of coerced "social change" that would gradually cause the disparate Tibetan tribal groups to unify and fight against their communist oppressors.

Mao's Strategy

Mao's approach to handling Tibet was to attempt to persuade the government of Tibet to accept a political agreement; he wanted to obtain the consent of the Dalai Lama to recognize China's sovereignty, which would reduce the risks of rebellion. For Mao, military intervention carried a moderate risk, although he did not anticipate any international intervention even if he had to resort to massive military force. On October 7, 1950, however, Mao ordered his troops to engage the poorly organized Tibetan army in Chamdo. The Tibetan army of 10,000 was soundly defeated in only two weeks and Tibet was essentially defenseless. This attack killed 4,000 Tibetan troops and intimidated the Dalai Lama into participating in negotiations with China. Meanwhile, Lhasa issued an appeal to the United Nations to settle the dispute (that Tibet is a state), but it was not considered. Tibetan officials traveled to Beijing and, following some inducements, signed the Seventeen-Point Agreement for the Peaceful Liberation of Tibet on May 23, 1951. The agreement nearly closed the "Tibet question": is Tibet an independent state or part of China? The answer for the Chinese was that Tibet had accepted political control by China. Essentially this agreement was consistent with Mao's gradualist policy to postpone major reforms in central Tibet until the populace became more willing to accept Chinese socialist changes.

The Prelude to the Rebellion

In the 1950s the People's Republic of China's new government initiated the first five-year plan and started the socialist transformation. Parts of eastern Tibet (Kham and Amdo) were subject to communist changes by 1952 and 1953. The Chinese considered Kham and Amdo as parts of provinces (Tsinghai, Szechwan, and Yunnan) established earlier and were not considered to be the central Tibetan region. The Chinese did not consider outlying areas as a part of the Seventeen-Point Agreement, even though Tibetans had inhabited the region for over five

The Tibetan Central Administration

The Tibetan Central Administration (TCA) is the leading official organization of Tibetan leaders outside of Tibet itself. Based in Dharamsala, India, the TCA is interested in aiding Tibetan refugees around the world, spreading awareness of the plight of Tibet under Chinese domination, and advocating for Tibetan freedom under a Tibetan government. The TCA is not a government in exile and is not recognized as such by other nations. It is organized by the Charter of the Tibetans in Exile, agreed upon in 1991.

At the heart of the Tibet Central Administration is the so-called Tibetan Parliament in Exile. Created by the Dalai Lama, it was largely designed to provide a model of democratic adminis-tration rather than any kind of direct government. The parliament consists of 43–46 members representing Tibet's regions as well as Tibetans living in other countries. It is headed by a speaker, who is elected from among the members of the parliament, and by a cabi-net of ministers who oversee matters including international rela-tions, finance, and religion and culture. In 2011, after years of laying groundwork, the Dalai Lama formally ceded all political authority over to the parliament.

The TCA's efforts in outreach have included the creation of a holiday known as Tibetan Uprising Day (commemorating the upris-ing of 1959), a Tibetan national anthem, and various fundraising efforts. It focuses particularly on the welfare and education of the nearly 100,000 Tibetans living in India.

centuries. Moreover, religiously speaking, both the Khampas and Amdowas (who later were key actors in the revolt) maintained devout patronage to the Dalai Lama as the sacred incarnation of Avalokitesvara (a compassionate Buddha).

In early 1953 certain areas in Kham were subjected to Chi-nese oppression. Thousands of monasteries were obliterated, lamas were sentenced to death, and monks sent to prison. These early Chinese initiatives reflect the socialist changes in the forced collectivization of agriculture, curtailing nomadic herding, atheist indoctrination, and the disarmament of the Tibetans. The reforms spread and soon afterward about 80,000 fiercely independent Khampas rose up in a rebellion against the Chinese. Again, in August 1954, 40,000 Tibetans rebelled in Kham, but the most serious rebellion was the Kanting rebellion of 1955–6, when Khampas engaged in violence against communist government bureaucrats and the Han Chinese. This was followed by yet another regional outbreak, the Szechwan Chando rebellion in 1956. Both groups were dispersed by mobilized Chinese armies and air force attacks that killed thousands of Khampans and Amdowas. By late 1956 the PLA dispersed Khampas, and Amdowas began trekking to Lhasa to seek refuge from PLA crackdowns and persecutions, as well as to protect their god-king, the Dalai Lama. In total, 15,000 rebels from eastern Tibet had settled in Lhasa. News of the Chinese aggression had become well known and posed a threat of impending violence in the capital.

The Rebellion in Lhasa, 1959

The Chinese presence in Lhasa and news of the brutal violence against rebels generated deep resentments. By 1954 a grassroots resistance group had began operations in Lhasa. Called the Mimang Tsongdu (People's Meetings), the group engaged in demonstrations and publicly hung posters criticizing the Chinese for their treatment of the Dalai Lama and their restrictions on Tibetan social observances and religious ceremonies. In 1957 the Chinese cracked down on the movement and imprisoned a number of its leaders. By then outer Tibet had been forcefully reorganized into 47 communes.

In 1958 fighting broke out in Lhoka, about 50 miles from Lhasa, as Khampas were pursued by the PLA, engaging the rebels on over a dozen occasions. As more rebels filtered into Lhasa, the Chinese infuriated the tribal leaders by attempting to expel them from the city. News of PLA interrogations of nomads across

Tibet revealed thousands of civilians were abusively treated by the PLA. With the Chinese continuing the pressure, a Kham-born merchant, Gompo Tashi Andrugstang, began organizing 23 tribal groups to unite and fight against the Chinese. Five thousand Khampas volunteered to join the newly formed military organization they called the Chushi Gandruk (Four Rivers and Six Ranges). The resistance movement formed its base of operations at Trighthang, 50 miles south of Lhasa. From August 1958 to April 1959 it reported 14 violent engagements against numerous PLA forces in the region, ranging in distances from 5 to 100 miles from Lhasa. This protracted and dispersed rebellion left no doubt that China had no intention of permitting the Tibetans political and religious freedom.

Although the Dalai Lama pleaded with the Khampas to cease their operations and settle their differences peacefully, the Chushi Gandruk continued fighting. The resistance fighters reported that the Chinese military used coordinated troop movements to set up ambush points. On April 14, 1959, the Khampa base was discovered and overrun, dispersing the Khampas, some of whom returned to Lhasa. The crowds in the city had increased; combined with the NVDA (National Volunteer Defense Army), they composed about 30,000 Khampas, Amdowas, and other tribal Tibetans. Lhasa was crowded and tense.

In February of 1959 a rumor began circulating that the Dalai Lama had been invited to a theater presentation by the PLA military leaders. The Tibetans, however, felt it was a Chinese ruse to kidnap the Dalai Lama. By March 10, the rumor had become magnified and created a veritable panic among the Tibetan faithful. It has been reported that over 20,000 Tibetans assembled around the palace and Chinese army headquarters. The crowd assembly whipped up further hatred for the Chinese, and a mob killed a Tibetan politician and injured a member of the Dalai Lama's cabinet. This incident further ignited the crowds for action. From mid-March to June, the Dalai Lama's palace was besieged with thousands of Tibetans who by now believed that their god-king was in mortal danger. By mid-June the situation in Lhasa was very tense and the PLA reinforced its defenses, waiting on the outskirts of the city. Artillery was brought in and set up around the perimeter. For the Dalai Lama, the rebellion was on his doorstep and his advisors began planning for his escape from possible arrest or worse by the Chinese authorities.

On June 14, recognizing that he could no longer influence the crowds, the Dalai Lama was disguised in military garb and escaped to India where he was immediately given political asylum. In his article "The Tibetan Rebellion of 1959 and China's Changing Relations with India and the Soviet Union" (2006), Jian shows that Mao was still coolly playing his game of strategy: he really did not care if the Dalai Lama escaped since it just changed the strategy. As the unfriendly crowds harassed PLA troops there, some groups became more violent; still their orders were to hold out but not engage the "rebels." However, by March 20

The Dalai Lama (center, on white pony) escapes into exile across the Himalayan mountains in 1959, following a failed Tibetan revolt against the Chinese occupation. © Popperfoto/Getty Images.

the PLA began attacking the Tibetans in Lhasa, opening fire with small arms, mortars, and artillery at rebel positions. The PLA also organized maneuvers around Lhasa and repeatedly engaged a fierce resistance until March 23. The PLA eventually crushed the rebellion, killing a total of 80,000 Tibetans between 1958 and 1959.

Following the rebellion, the CIA (US Central Intelligence Agency) funded air drops to Tibetan guerillas to ascertain the possibility of maintaining the resistance. During the escape of the Dalai Lama in 1959, CIA operatives assisted in making advanced requests for his political asylum. While a number of incursions have been reported, there was no appreciable effect of their clandestine activity.

The Dalai Lama set up his government-in-exile in Dharamsala, India, condemning the Seventeen-Point Agreement and pleading for Tibetan independence. Soon after the Dalai Lama arrived, thousands of faithful pilgrims also crossed the border to join him.

Causes of the Rebellion

While the communist plan was an initial success, failure was ultimately linked to the Chinese assumption that outer Tibet was part of China. This region was subject to more immediate communist transformation that involved disregard for the symbols of religion signified by Tibetan monks and monasteries. In his 1979 article "The 1959 Tibetan Rebellion: An Interpretation," Dawa Norbu argues that the Tibetans had become painfully aware of what the socialist transformation meant, and when surrounding tribal groups filled Lhasa, the atmosphere was volatile.

A related factor in the rebellion was the outrage felt by Tibetans in Lhasa at the early abuse of Khampas and Amdowas in which brutality was displayed (during the democratic reforms in eastern Tibet). The casualties inflicted between 1953 and 1958 were in the thousands: the Chinese air force devastated rebels, nomad civilians, homes, livestock, and monasteries, but there was a lag in the realization of the devastation given the expanse and isolation of the region. It also offended the Buddhists, for instance, when the Chinese treated nuns, monks, and lamas with disdain and meted out draconian punishments—an affront to their religious faith. As the PLA smashed the Khampa rebels, the cause also became one of protecting their way of life and their religious leader.

In addition, there are causal wildcards that appear plausible: rumors in Lhasa may also have played a role in generating mass anxiety and anger in the crowds, as did the artillery explosions near the Norbulinka (Jian considered them accidental) that energized their gathering and precipitated murder in rebellious defiance for a week before the PLA crackdown on June 20. In the end, Goldstein and Norbu agree that Mao failed in his gradualist approach by oppressing eastern Tibetans, whom he did not comprehend. Moreover, after he reached India, the Dalai Lama once again raised the issue of declaring Tibet's independence from China.

References and Suggested Readings

Goldstein, M. (1997) *The Snow Lion and the Dragon: China, Tibet, and the Dalai Lama.* Berkeley: University of California Press.

Jian, C. (2006) The Tibetan Rebellion of 1959 and China's Changing Relations with India and the Soviet Union. *Journal of Cold War Studies* 8, 3 (Summer).

McGranahan, C. (2006) The CIA and the Chushi Gandrug Resistance, 1956–1974. *Journal of Cold War Studies* 8, 3 (Summer).

Norbu, D. (1979) The 1959 Tibetan Rebellion: An Interpretation. *China Quarterly* (March).

Patterson, G. (1960) China and Tibet: Background to the Revolt. *China Quarterly* (January–March).

Tibetan Resistance Fighters Receive Training and Aid from the United States

Carole McGranahan

In the 1950s, when Communist China asserted its control over Tibet, the Cold War in Asia was beginning to take shape. The United States committed itself to stopping the spread of communism in Asia just as it had in Europe. One form this effort took was containing the influence of the major communist powers: China in Asia and the Soviet Union in Europe. In the following viewpoint, scholar Carole McGranahan explores how Tibet almost inevitably became involved in Cold War politics. She describes how some anti-Chinese Tibetan rebels received assistance and arms from American interests; some even traveled to the state of Colorado for military training. One of the goals of these Tibetan fighters, she suggests, was the protection and possible exile of the Dalai Lama, Tibet's spiritual and political leader. McGranahan also notes how US involvement drew the country further into the complex political and cultural issues surrounding the fluid border regions of the Himalayas—where states such as India, Pakistan, and Nepal pursue their own interests, as well as China and Tibet. McGranahan is professor of anthropology at the University of Colorado, Boulder, and the author of Arrested Histories: Tibet, the CIA, and the Histories of a Forgotten War, *and many scholarly articles on Tibet.*

Colorado's mountain roads can be treacherous in the winter, and in December 1961 a bus crashed on an icy road in the middle of the night. The crash delayed the bus's journey, and morning had already broken by the time the bus pulled into its destination, Peterson Airfield in Colorado Springs. The coffee had just begun to brew when airfield workers discovered that they were surrounded by heavily-armed U.S. soldiers. The troops ordered them into two different hangars and then shut and locked the doors. Peeking out the windows of the hangars, the airfield employees saw a bus with blackened windows pull up to a waiting Air Force plane. Fifteen men in green fatigues got out of the bus and onto the plane. After the aircraft took off, an Army officer informed the airfield employees that it was a federal offense to talk about what they had just witnessed. He swore them to the highest secrecy, but it was already too late: The hangars in which the scared civilians had been locked were equipped with telephones, and they had made several calls to local newspapers. The next day the *Colorado Springs Gazette Telegraph* ran a brief story quoting a student pilot who said that "several Oriental soldiers in combat uniforms" were involved. The short story caught the attention of a *New York Times* reporter in Washington, DC, who called the Pentagon for more information. His call was returned by Secretary of Defense Robert McNamara, who killed the story not only by uttering the words "top secret national security," but also by confiding to the reporter that the men were Tibetans.

A Tibetan proverb states that "an unspoken word has freedom, a spoken word has none." But the freedom of things unspoken is not without limits. Secrets, for example, though supposedly not to be told, derive their value in part by being shared rather than being kept. Sharing secrets—revealing the unspoken—often involves cultural systems of regulation regarding who can be told, who they in turn can tell, what degree of disclosure is allowed, and so on. As a form of control over knowledge, secrecy is recognized in many societies as a means through which power is both gained and maintained. Together, Tibet and the U.S. Central Intelligence Agency (CIA) present the irresistible combination of two twentieth-century icons of forbidden mystery and intrigue—Tibet, Shangri-La, the supposed land of mystical and ancient wisdom; and the CIA, home of covert activities, where even the secrets have secrets.

Training a Resistance Group

The Tibetans in Colorado were members of a guerrilla resistance force that fought against the Chinese People's Liberation Army (PLA) from 1956 through 1974. Begun as a series of independent uprisings against increasingly oppressive Chinese rule, the resistance soon grew into a unified volunteer army, known as the Chushi Gangdrug Army. The Chushi Gangdrug Army fought against the PLA first from within Tibet and later from a military base in Mustang, a small Tibetan kingdom within the borders of Nepal. For much of this time, the resistance was covertly trained and financially supported by the U.S. government, specifically the CIA. Stories of this guerrilla war were secret for many years. Because the operation encompassed multiple governments and the clandestine transfer of men, money, and munitions across international borders, it is perhaps no surprise that information about the resistance, and more specifically about U.S.-Tibetan relations, was suppressed until recently. Secrets of the Tibetan resistance, however, are not always as they appear. They are not only political but also ethnographic, built on cultural systems of meaning and action. . . .

United States Involvement with Tibet

The United States and Tibet do not have a long history of governmental relations. Contact was first made under President Franklin Roosevelt in 1942, shortly after the United States had entered World War II. The U.S. government wanted to transport supplies over and through Tibet to troops in China. Roosevelt sent two undercover Office of Strategic Services envoys to Lhasa to seek approval. The mission was successful, but the next interaction between the two countries did not come until 1947–1948 when a Tibetan trade mission, traveling on Tibetan passports, came to the United States as part of a global mission to strengthen Tibet's international economic and political relations at a time of growing political pressure from China.

With the Communist takeover in China in 1949, U.S. interest in Tibet grew exponentially. Histories of the Tibetan resistance, therefore, are not just Tibetan histories but a part of the broader history of the Cold War. Tibet had an important role in U.S. Cold War strategy in Asia as both a counter to Communist China and a facilitator of U.S. relations with Pakistan and India. Although many Americans who were politically involved with Tibet at this time developed strong personal support for the Tibetans, Tibet remained for the U.S. government, as it had been for the British, a "pawn on the imperial chessboard." The Tibetans themselves, to use the words of a former CIA officer, were thus "orphans of the Cold War."

South Asia was never divorced from Cold War politics. The departure of the British from India in 1947 led to the partition of the subcontinent and the emergence of the independent states of India and Pakistan. The two countries were quickly embroiled in a contentious dispute with each other and were also pulled into Cold War battles involving the United States, the Soviet Union, and the PRC. Pakistan was first closely linked with the United States and then later on with China. India took a different route, publicly proclaiming a nonaligned status while secretly courting and being courted by Washington, Moscow, and Beijing. The secretive, constantly changing, and often contradictory allegiances among governments in the 1950s and 1960s resulted in several armed conflicts—the Sino-Indian War of 1962, the Indo-Pakistani War of 1965, the ongoing insurgency in Kashmir, and the Tibetan conflict with China.

Border Concerns: Tibet, China, India, and Pakistan

It was China that pulled South Asia into the Cold War, often over border disputes involving Tibet. Tibet's new status as an occupied country and a site of Cold War conflict was a significant departure from its status in the preceding fifty years. During the first half of the twentieth century, Tibet kept a low international profile. Its affiliation with China, based on a religious-political relationship, ended when the Qing Dynasty fell. From 1911 on, Tibet was an independent state, uninvolved in any of the world wars but ideologically and religiously supporting the Allies in World War II. In turn, the British and later the Americans encouraged Tibetan political independence, though only to the point where it would not seriously upset China. Despite ideological and other differences between successive Chinese regimes, each was interested in bringing Tibet within the Chinese political orbit. Mao Zedong's China was no different in that respect.

From the start, Mao announced that his intention was to "liberate" Tibet and restore it to the Chinese motherland. He was true to his word—Chinese troops entered eastern Tibet in the spring of 1950 and quickly secured control over all of Tibet by occupying Lhasa in the fall of 1950. After an initial period of attempted cooperation with the Chinese, the situation disintegrated rapidly for the Tibetans. In eastern Tibet, people began a series of independent revolts, which the Chinese brutally suppressed using air strikes and ground warfare. The U.S. government had offered aid to the Tibetan government after China invaded, and the Tibetans asked the United States for military aid in 1955. The CIA established its Tibet program the next year. An initial group of six Tibetans were trained on the island of Saipan and then air-dropped into Tibet. In the meantime, the previously independent groups of Tibetans who had been fighting the Chinese were brought into the united resistance movement. CIA training of Tibetan soldiers continued in the United States, first at a secret site in Virginia and then, starting in May 1958, at the equally secret Camp Hale in Leadville, Colorado. Over the next six years, several hundred Tibetans were trained at Camp Hale in a variety of guerrilla warfare techniques such as paramilitary operations, bomb building, map making, photographic surveillance, radio operation techniques, and intelligence collection.

"The [Tibetans] were the best men I worked with," says Tony Poe, a retired CIA officer who trained the Tibetan soldiers and later worked in Laos. Poe is believed to be the real-life model for the character of Kurtz in [the Vietnam War film] *Apocalypse Now*. He and the other American instructors are remembered fondly by the Tibetans themselves. "They were good people" (*mi yag po red*) is a common refrain I heard during my research. Despite the mutual admiration of the Tibetans and Americans, a series of misunderstandings marred the relationship. The United States was mainly interested in preventing the spread of Communism rather than providing serious and committed aid to Tibet. . . .

A Critical Discovery

In November 1961, CIA Director Allen Dulles appeared at a meeting of the U.S. National Security Council's Special Group carrying an unusual item—the bloodstained and bullet-riddled pouch of a Chinese army commander. No less graphic than the pouch was what it contained—more than 1,600 classified Chinese documents described as not merely an "intelligence goldmine" but "the best intelligence coup since the Korean War." The pouch and documents were well traveled, having been carried on foot by Tibetan guerrillas out of Tibet through Nepal and into India, where they were whisked away to the United States on transport aircraft. The Tibetan soldiers who captured the documents were part of the Chushi Gangdrug volunteer army's Mustang force.

The Tibetans did not enjoy uniform support in Washington. In the early 1960s, with the transition from the [Dwight D.] Eisenhower to the [John F.] Kennedy administration, senior officials debated whether the covert operation in Tibet should be continued. Allen Dulles' dramatic introduction of the bloodstained bag literally "shot through with explanation" could not have been better timed. The documents in the pouch were of priceless value to the U.S. government. At the time, little intelligence information existed about the PRC. China presented itself as a perfectly functioning state, one that was militarily secure, with a population that was flourishing. The documents revealed just the opposite: that the Great Leap Forward [a Chinese attempt at forced economic development from 1958 to 1961] had failed catastrophically and had led to widespread famine in China, and that serious internal problems had arisen in the military and the party. The importance of these documents to the CIA was unparalleled, and the scholarly community responded in kind when the materials were released several years later. Nowhere, however, was it revealed how the U.S. government had obtained the documents. Although President John F. Kennedy approved the continuation of the Tibetan project, the story of the men who captured the documents remained a secret.

The Tibetan government was also interested in the documents, though for a different reason. After leaving Lhasa, the only evidence the Tibetan government could obtain of the atrocities committed by Chinese troops was the oral testimony of Tibetan refugees. These testimonies were valuable but not as valuable as hard documentary evidence. The materials captured by the guerrillas contained crucial and tragic confirmation of the magnitude of violence in Tibet. The documents showed that in Lhasa alone more than 87,000 Tibetans had been killed by the Chinese military from March 1959 through September 1960. This evidence of Chinese atrocities was invaluable for the Tibetan government when it presented its case in the diplomatic language of international law. For the Tibetan government-in-exile, as for the CIA, the substance of the documents was what mattered rather than tales of how and by whom they had been obtained. The Dalai Lama's autobiography, published in 1990, indicates that the documents were "captured by Tibetan freedom fighters during the 1960s."

Considering the importance accorded to the documents by the U.S. and Tibetan governments, one might expect that the former guerrillas would highlight this event in their narrations of resistance history. But as I soon found, this is not the case at all. They neither begin nor end their accounts with any mention of the documents, and they often did not refer to them at all. Why is it that this particular achievement so valued by the U.S. and Tibetan governments, is hot remotely as memorable for the former soldiers?

The Tibetan Goal Was to Return Home Independent

Following the 1959 Tibetan exodus into South Asia, the resistance operated out of Mustang, the ethnic Tibetan kingdom that jutted up from the borders of northern Nepal into Tibet. In Mustang, the men established camps from which they could periodically sneak across the border into Tibet, raiding army camps, dynamiting roads, stealing animals, and collecting information and transmitting it by radio to the United States. One of their goals was to ambush PLA convoys, kill the soldiers, and confiscate all their weapons, supplies, and materials. On one especially successful raid they captured a large pouch stuffed with documents. The documents were all in Chinese, a language that none of the Tibetans could read. A veteran named Lobsang Jampa was one of the few who did mention the documents to me. He recalled:

> There was a man called Gen Rara. He was very popular among us. He led an attack on the Chinese and secured some very important documents from a Chinese official. This proved very useful to us. . . . We sent those documents on. But I don't know what they were about.

Other veterans who referred to the documents were similarly nonplussed. In Pokhara, Wangyal Lama explained, "our soldiers attacked Chinese trucks and seized some documents of the Chinese government. After that the Americans increased our pay scale. Nobody knew what the contents of those documents were. At that time, questions weren't asked. If you asked too many questions, others would be suspicious of you." Baba Yeshi, the general who was in charge of operations in Mustang, said that:

> A group of thirty Tibetans on horse traveled into Tibet. . . . Nine days later the group returned with uniforms, hats, diaries, Chinese government documents, and a lot of ammunition. . . . All that was captured resulted from the ambush of two Chinese convoys in western Tibet. [I] sent the diaries and government documents to Darjeeling. . . . [Later] four CIA officials congratulated me on overcoming such difficult initial conditions and praised me for our success in attacking the Chinese. As a reward the CIA gave me an Omega chronograph.

Apparently, the Americans did not realize that the Tibetans had discriminating tastes in timepieces. [Ethnic] Khampas had dominated the transnational Tibetan trade industry, and many of the resistance soldiers were former traders who possessed a sophisticated knowledge of the market value (and not just the use value) of international commodities. On this topic, Lobsang Jampa adds that at an earlier time "we were also given Omega wrist watches by the American instructors. They also gave us one trunk full of other watches. These watches were of cheap quality, and some of our soldiers did not want them." What the soldiers *did* want was the restoration of Tibet to the rule of the Dalai Lama and the opportunity to return to their homes—that is, for life to return to "normal." Captured documents of unknown importance were but a small victory and, at that particular moment, difficult to regard as a concrete step toward their goal. . . .

Secrets Told and Untold

The story of the "Colorado Tibetans" that opened this article is an example of how the story of the resistance as a government secret dominates the literature on the CIA-Tibet connection. As words not quite "unspoken," but spoken only to a select few, secrets have the freedom and the license to travel, circulating not just as acknowledged silences but also as truths to be pursued and revealed. Thus, although many Tibetans feel obliged not to divulge resistance secrets, outsiders are not bound by the same constraints. In the late 1960s and early 1970s, despite the best efforts of the U.S. and Tibetan governments to keep things under wraps, bits and pieces of what was going on began to slip out. A series of investigative and speculative articles appeared, some romanticizing the resistance and others criticizing the CIA, the Tibetan government, or both. Currently, the literature in both English and Tibetan on the resistance is growing, albeit along somewhat different tracks and in both cases giving away some secrets while still keeping others.

Admittedly, guerrilla resistance and government intelligence work are, by their very nature, secretive enterprises. In this case, the history is doubly secret because of the international political climate at the time—the height of the Cold War—and because independence remains an elusive goal for the Tibetan resistance and exile community. Only recently did the U.S. government begin releasing information about its involvement with the Tibetan resistance. In Asia, even less official information is available. The Nepalese government publicly denied any knowledge, not to mention approval, of the Tibetans' use of Nepalese territory for resistance operations. Privately, however, the King of Nepal had told the U.S. government as far back as 1950 that he was willing to aid the Tibetans. In India today, the public knows little about its government's cooperation with the United States in aiding the Tibet resistance.

Indeed, not until April 1978, when rumors began to circulate that the Ganges, the most sacred river in India, had been polluted by the government, was there even the slightest public hint of India's role vis-à-vis Tibet. The Indian government caused a stir when it acknowledged that the rumors might be true. It turned out that India and the United States had conducted a series of secret operations against China in 1965, including the installation of plutonium-239 devices to monitor Chinese missile launches and nuclear explosions on the high reaches of the Himalayan peak of Nanda Devi. Later, when intelligence teams went to retrieve the sensors, a 33-pound pack containing two to three pounds of plutonium could not be found. Intelligence officials assumed—rightly, as it turned out—that the monitors had been swept away by an avalanche and had perhaps ended up in the Ganges River, which runs past Nanda Devi.

Other secrets are only beginning to come to light, such as the revelation that the Tibetan resistance provided key intelligence information to the U.S. government, including information about PLA military capacity, internal dissent in China during the Great Leap Forward, and information about the first Chinese nuclear tests at Lop Nor in northern Tibet. Secrets between governments persist and are a key part of the history of the resistance, yet what for India, Pakistan, Nepal, and the United States was an official secret, was for the Tibetans much more. For the Tibetan community, the story of the resistance is not just one of clandestine politics or government secrets; rather, it consists of multiple stories—personal tales of serving the nation and the Dalai Lama, accounts of the armed struggle for their country, and continuing debates over facets of communal identity in the exile community.

The resistance was ultimately unsuccessful in regaining Tibet, but that does not diminish its historical importance for the resistance movement. Many Chushi Gangdrug veterans consider the resistance a key part of recent Tibetan history and view their own combat experiences as defining moments in their lives. For veterans, the resistance was important in defending Tibet against the Chinese and in defending and protecting the Dalai Lama in his escape from Tibet.

A United Nations Committee Reports That China Has Committed Acts of Genocide in Tibet

International Commission of Jurists

The problem of Tibet began to achieve widespread global attention in the aftermath of the defeated 1959 uprising that sent the Dalai Lama into exile in India. In the following viewpoint, a commission of legal experts connected to the United Nations reports on various offenses allegedly committed by Chinese officials before and during the uprising. These offenses included strict limitations of personal freedom, the uprooting of thousands from their homes, and numerous attacks on Tibetan Buddhism, ranging from the targeting of monasteries to the killing and intimidation of monks and believers. The commission concluded that such efforts were acts of genocide against the Tibetan people and their distinct culture, even though there was no widespread attempt at large-scale massacres.

The Legal Inquiry Committee on Tibet has the pleasure to submit to the International Commission of Jurists its Report on those aspects of events in Tibet which the Committee was called upon by its terms of reference to consider. The Committee came to the following conclusions:

According to the Convention for the Prevention and Punishment of Genocide, which was adopted by the General Assembly of the United Nations in December, 1948, human groups against which genocide is recognized as a crime in international law are national, racial, ethnic and religious. The *committee* found that acts of genocide had been committed in Tibet in an attempt to destroy the Tibetans as a religious group, and that such acts are acts of genocide independently of any conventional obligation. The *committee* did not find that there was sufficient proof of the destruction of Tibetans as a race, nation or ethnic group as such by methods that can be regarded as genocide in international law. The evidence established four principal facts in relation to genocide:

(a) that the Chinese will not permit adherence to and practice of Buddhism in Tibet;

(b) that they have systematically set out to eradicate this religious belief in Tibet;

(c) that in pursuit of this design they have killed religious figures because their religious belief and practice was an encouragement and example to others; and

(d) that they have forcibly transferred large numbers of Tibetan children to a Chinese materialist environment in order to prevent them from having a religious upbringing.

The *committee* therefore found that genocide had been committed against this religious group by such methods.

The Violation of Human Rights

The *committee* examined evidence in relation to human rights within the framework of the Universal Declaration of Human Rights as proclaimed by the General Assembly of the United Nations.

The *committee* in considering the question of human rights took into account that economic and social rights are as much

Monks protest in front of the United Nations building in New York City in 1959, shortly after the Dalai Lama's forced exile from Tibet. © Carl Mydans/Time Life Pictures/Getty Images.

a part of human rights as are civil liberties. They found that the Chinese communist authorities in Tibet had violated human rights of both kinds.

The *committee* came to the conclusion that the Chinese authorities in Tibet had violated the following human rights, which the *committee* considered to be the standards of behavior in the common opinion of civilized nations:

Article 3. The right to life, liberty and security of person was violated by acts of murder, rape and arbitrary imprisonment.

Article 5. Torture and cruel, inhuman and degrading treatment were inflicted on the Tibetans on a large scale.

Article 9. Arbitrary arrests and detention were carried out.

Article 12. Rights of privacy, of home and family life were persistently violated by the forcible transfer of members of the family and by indoctrination turning children against their parents.

Children from infancy upwards were removed contrary to the wishes of the parents.

Article 13. Freedom of movement within, to and from Tibet was denied by large-scale deportations.

Article 16. The voluntary nature of marriage was denied by forcing monks and lamas to marry.

Article 17. The right not to be arbitrarily deprived of private property was violated by the confiscation and compulsory acquisition of private property otherwise than on payment of just compensation and in accordance with the freely expressed wish of the Tibetan People.

Article 18. Freedom of thought, conscience and religion were denied by acts of genocide against Buddhists in Tibet and by other systematic acts designed to eradicate religious belief in Tibet.

Article 19. Freedom of expression and opinion was denied by the destruction of scriptures, the imprisonment of members of the Mimang group [a people's resistance organization] and the cruel punishments inflicted on critics of the regime.

Article 20. The right of free assembly and association was violated by the suppression of the Mimang movement and the prohibition of meetings other than those called by the Chinese.

Article 21. The right to democratic government was denied by the imposition from outside of rule by and under the Chinese Communist Party.

Article 22. The economic, social and cultural rights indispensable for the dignity and free development of the personality of man were denied. The economic resources of Tibet were used to meet the needs of the Chinese. Social changes were adverse to the interests of the majority of the Tibetan people. The old culture of Tibet, including its religion, was attacked in an attempt to eradicate it.

Article 24. The right to reasonable working conditions was violated by the exaction of labor under harsh and ill-paid conditions.

Article 25. A reasonable standard of living was denied by the use of the Tibetan economy to meet the needs of the Chinese settling in Tibet.

Article 26. The right to liberal education primarily in accordance with the choice of parents was denied by compulsory indoctrination, sometimes after deportation, in communist philosophy.

Article 27. The Tibetans were not allowed to participate in the cultural life of their own community, a culture which the Chinese have set out to destroy.

Chinese allegations that the Tibetans enjoyed no human rights before the entry of the Chinese were found to be based on distorted and exaggerated accounts of life in Tibet. Accusations against the Tibetan "rebels" of rape, plunder and torture were found in cases of plunder to have been deliberately fabricated and in other cases unworthy of belief for this and other reasons.

The Status of Tibet

The view of the *committee* was that Tibet was at the very least a de facto independent State when the Agreement of Peaceful Measures in Tibet was signed in 1951, and the repudiation of this agreement by the Tibetan Government in 1959 was found to be fully justified. In examining the evidence, the *committee* took into account events in Tibet as related in authoritative accounts by officials and scholars familiar at first hand with the recent history of Tibet and official documents which have been

China's Cultural Revolution

Beginning in 1966 supporters of aging Chinese Communist leader Mao Zedong inaugurated a so-called Great Proletarian Cultural Revolution. Their hope was to revive the revolutionary momentum that had placed the Communists in control in China back in 1949. Their methods included an attempted transformation of Chinese society, but results included an alleged hundreds of thousands of deaths and imprisonments, the destruction of centuries-old monuments and treasures, and the targeting of ethnic minorities such as Tibetans.

During the Cultural Revolution, students were put in charge of classrooms, children were encouraged to inform on their parents, and city-dwellers and educated people were sent down to the countryside to work on state-run farms. Most active among the revolutionaries were so-called Red Guards, usually groups of young people inspired to revolutionary enthusiasm by Mao's *Little Red Book* of collected sayings. The Red Guards often staged destructive demonstrations and even riots, targeting any who did not seem to be revolutionary enough. These included those who might be too interested in China's imperial history; "capitalist running dogs" who favored the free market over a state-controlled economy; and, again, ethnic minority groups. Red Guards ransacked or destroyed as many as 6,000 Tibetan monasteries while ordinary Tibetans were strongly pressured to abandon their traditional faith and ways of life. This pressure included beatings and imprisonment.

The Cultural Revolution wound down in the early 1970s as Chinese leaders came to understand how excessive and destructive it had been. It is finally thought to have ended with the death of Mao Zedong in 1976, a development which eventually opened the way for China's rapid economic growth in the 1980s, 1990s, and first decades of the twenty-first century.

published. These show that Tibet demonstrated from 1913 to 1950 the conditions of statehood as generally accepted under international law. In 1950 there was a people and a territory, and a government which functioned in that territory, conducting its own domestic affairs free from any outside authority. From 1913–1950 foreign relations or Tibet were conducted exclusively by the Government of Tibet and countries with whom Tibet had foreign relations are shown by official documents to have treated Tibet in practice as an independent State.

Tibet surrendered her independence by signing in 1951 the Agreement on Peaceful Measures for the Liberation of Tibet. Under that Agreement the Central People's Government of the Chinese People's Republic gave a number of undertakings, among them: promises to maintain the existing political system of Tibet, to maintain the status and functions of the Dalai Lama and the Panchen Lama [political and religious leaders], to protect freedom of religion and the monasteries and to refrain from compulsion in the matter of reforms in Tibet. The *committee* found that these and other undertakings had been violated by the Chinese People's Republic, and that the Government of Tibet was entitled to repudiate the Agreement as it did on March 11, 1959.

On the status of Tibet the previous inquiry was limited to considering whether the question of Tibet was a matter essentially within the domestic jurisdiction of the Chinese People's Republic. The *committee* considered that it should confine itself to this question and it was therefore not necessary to attempt a definitive analysis in terms of modern international law of the exact juridical status of Tibet. The *committee* was not concerned with the question whether the status of Tibet in 1950 was one of de facto [in practice] or de jure [in law] independence and was satisfied that Tibet's status was such as to make the Tibetan question one for the legitimate concern of the United Nations even on the restrictive interpretation of matters "essentially within the domestic jurisdiction" of a State.

Tibet's Leader, the Dalai Lama, Explains His Exile

The Dalai Lama

Ever since the 1300s a figure known as the Dalai Lama has been one of the most prominent people in Tibet. In Tibetan Buddhism he is considered to be a reincarnation of a Buddha of compassion known as Avalokitesvara, and he serves as head of a major school of the faith, the so-called Yellow Hat school. In addition, at various points in history the Dalai Lama has served as the political leader of Tibet. The title, roughly translated from an ancient Mongolian language, means "ocean of wisdom." The current Dalai Lama, who has the given name of Tenzin Gyatso, has held the title since before the Chinese takeover in 1951. During the 1950s when the first Tibetan uprisings began, he was also the chief administrator of what the Chinese called the Tibetan Autonomous Region. During the 1959 anti-Chinese uprising, when in response Chinese officials targeted Buddhist officials, sites, and rituals specifically, the Dalai Lama chose to go into exile. In the following viewpoint, he explains his thinking, through official spokesmen, to journalists from around the world. Welcomed by the Government of India, the Dalai Lama eventually set up a Tibetan government-in-exile based in the northern Indian town of Dharamsala. While in 2011

The Dalai Lama, "The Dalai Lama's Press Statements: Statements Issued at Tezpur," claudearpi.net, April 18, 1959. Reproduced by permission.

he gave up any claim to political leadership, the Dalai Lama continues to advocate on behalf of Tibetans worldwide and for peace in general.

It has always been accepted that the Tibetan people are different from the Han [mainstream] people of China. There has always been a strong desire for independence on the part of the Tibetan people. Throughout history this has been asserted on numerous occasions. Sometimes, the Chinese Government have imposed their suzerainty on Tibet and, at other times, Tibet has functioned as an independent country. In any event, at all times, even when the suzerainty of China was imposed, Tibet remained autonomous in control of its internal affairs.

In 1951, under pressure of the Chinese Government, a 17-Point Agreement was made between China and Tibet. In that Agreement, the suzerainty of China was accepted as there was no alternative left to the Tibetans. But even in the Agreement, it was stated that Tibet would enjoy full autonomy. Though the control of External Affairs and Defence were to be in the hands of the Chinese Government, it was agreed that there would be no interference by the Chinese Government with the Tibetan religion and customs and her internal administration. In fact, after the occupation of Tibet by the Chinese armies, the Tibetan Government did not enjoy any measure of autonomy even in internal matters, and the Chinese Government exercised full powers in Tibet's affairs. In 1956, a Preparatory Committee was set up for Tibet with the Dalai Lama as Chairman, the Panchen Lama as Vice-Chairman and General Chang Kuo Hun as the Representative of the Chinese Government. In practice, even this body had little power, and decisions in all important matters were taken by the Chinese authorities. The Dalai Lama and his Government tried their best to adhere to the 17-Point Agreement, but the interference of the Chinese authorities persisted.

By the end of 1955 a struggle had started in the Kham Province and this assumed serious proportions in 1956. In the

Tibet's Dalai Lamas

For hundreds of years Tibet's primary spiritual and political leader has been a figure known as the Dalai Lama, a Mongolian phrase that means "ocean of wisdom." The current Dalai Lama is the fourteenth in a line that stretches back to the fourteenth century.

The office of Dalai Lama emerged when Tibetan Buddhism became more institutionalized in the fourteenth century. The Yellow Hat sect emerged as the dominant school within the faith, while the Red Hat sect became its main competitor. The first four Dalai Lamas were primarily heads of monasteries and leading religious figures. But the fifth Dalai Lama, who lived from 1617 to 1682, combined religious and political leadership. He established Yellow Hat Buddhism as the main state religion; built the Potala Palace in Lhasa, Tibet's capital; and helped the faith spread beyond the nation's borders to parts of China, Russia, and India. Subsequent Dalai Lamas continued with their political involvement to different degrees.

consequential struggle, the Chinese Armed Forces destroyed a large number of monasteries. Many Lamas were killed and a large number of monks and officials were taken and employed on the construction of roads in China, and the interference in the exercise of religious freedom increased.

The relations of Tibetans with China became openly strained from the early part of February, 1959. The Dalai Lama had agreed a month in advance to attend a cultural show in the Chinese headquarters and the date was suddenly fixed for the 10th of March. The people of Lhasa [Tibet's capital and only big city] became apprehensive that some harm might be done to the Dalai Lama and as a result about ten thousand people gathered round the Dalai Lama's summer palace, Norbulingka, and physically prevented the Dalai Lama from attending the function. Thereafter, the people themselves decided to raise a bodyguard for the protection of the Dalai Lama. Large crowds of Tibetans went about the streets

The source of the Dalai Lama's authority is religious. Tibetan Buddhists believe that the Dalai Lama is the reincarnation of all earlier Dalai Lamas as well as a bodhisattva, or enlightened soul, called Avalokitesvara. He is therefore a "living Buddha." At the death of each Dalai Lama other "lamas," or religious teachers, begin a search for his successor. Any candidate must have been born 49 days after the previous Dalai Lama's death, be familiar with his possessions, and show signs of religious wisdom.

The current Dalai Lama, whose given name is Tenzin Gyatso, went into exile in India in 1959. He has advocated not only for the cause of Tibetan Buddhism but also for Tibetan freedom from Chinese control. A globally recognized figure of peace and nonviolence, he received the Nobel Peace Prize in 1989. Breaking with his predecessors, the current Dalai Lama gave up his position as the Tibetan head of state in 2011, ceding that authority to the Tibetan Parliament-in-Exile in India.

of Lhasa demonstrating against the Chinese rule in Tibet. Two days later, thousands of Tibetan women held demonstrations protesting against Chinese authority. In spite of this demonstration from the people, the Dalai Lama and his Government endeavoured to maintain friendly relations with the Chinese and tried to carry out negotiations with the Chinese representatives as to how best to bring about peace in Tibet and assuage the people's anxiety. While these negotiations were being carried out, reinforcements arrived to strengthen the Chinese garrisons in Lhasa and Tibet. On the 17th March, two or three mortar shells were fired in the direction of the Norbulingka Palace. Fortunately, the shells fell in a nearby pond. After this, the Advisers became alive to the danger to the person of the Dalai Lama and in those difficult circumstances it became imperative for the Dalai Lama, the members of his family and his high officials to leave Lhasa. The Dalai Lama would like to state categorically that he left Lhasa and Tibet and came to India of his own free will and not under duress.

It was due to the loyalty and affectionate support of his people that the Dalai Lama was able to find his way through a route which is quite arduous. The route which the Dalai Lama took involved the Kyichu and the Tsangpo rivers and making his way through Lhoka area, Yarlung Valley and Tsona Dzong before reaching the Indian Frontier at Kanzey Mane near Chut hangmu.

On the 29th March, 1959, the Dalai Lama sent two emissaries across the Indo-Tibetan border requesting Government of India's permission to enter India and seek asylum there. The Dalai Lama is extremely grateful to the people and Government of India for their spontaneous and generous welcome as well as the asylum granted to him and his followers. India and Tibet have religious, cultural and trade links extending over a thousand years and for Tibetans it has always been the land of enlightenment, having given birth to Lord Buddha. The Dalai Lama is deeply touched by the kind greeting extended to him on his safe arrival in India by the Prime Minister Shri Jawaharlal Nehru, and his colleagues in the Government of India. The Dalai Lama has already sent reply to this message of greetings.

Ever since the Dalai Lama entered India at Kanzey Mane, near Chuthangmu, he has experienced in full measure the respect and hospitality extended to him by the people of the Kameng Frontier Division of the North East Frontier Agency and the Dalai Lama would like to state how the Government of India's officers posted there had spared no efforts in making his stay and journey through this extremely well-administered part of India as comfortable as possible.

The Dalai Lama will now be proceeding to Mussoorie which he hopes to reach in the next few days. The Dalai Lama will give thought to his future plans and, if necessary, give expression to them as soon as he has had a chance to rest and reflect on recent events. His country and people have passed through an extremely

Tenzin Gyatso, the fourteenth Dalai Lama, is pictured in India in 1959, the year he was forced into exile. He remains in exile in Dharamsala, India. © Keystone Features/Getty Images.

difficult period and all that the Dalai Lama wishes to say at the moment is to express his sincere regrets at the tragedy which has overtaken Tibet and to fervently hope that these troubles would be over soon without any more bloodshed.

As the Dalai Lama and the spiritual head of all the Buddhists in Tibet, his foremost concern is the well-being of his people and in ensuring the perpetual flourishing of his sacred religion and freedom of his country.

While expressing once again thankfulness at his safe arrival in India, the Dalai Lama would like to take this opportunity to communicate to all his friends, well-wishers and devotees in India and abroad his sincere gratitude for the many messages of sympathies and concern with which they have flooded him.

The Opening of a Railway Line to Tibet's Capital Spurs Protests

Jehangir S. Pocha

One of the hallmarks of Tibetan culture has been the area's isolation. Separated from India to the south by the Himalayan Mountains and from most of China to the east by vast deserts, Tibet has always been difficult to reach. That began to change only in the midtwentieth century with the advent of long-distance highways and air travel. In the following viewpoint, journalist Jehangir S. Pocha records yet another change marking the end of Tibet's long isolation: the 2006 completion of a railway connecting China's capital, Beijing, to Lhasa, Tibet's former capital. While Chinese officials claim that the railway will help with the region's economic development, Tibetan and other protesters disagree. They argue that the new railroad will simply make it easier for China to impose its own way of life on Tibet, further displacing and marginalizing Tibetan culture. Pocha served as the China correspondent for the Boston Globe *before becoming editor of India's* Businessworld *magazine.*

In a rare protest by foreigners here, three Western activists who oppose China's new rail link to Tibet clambered up the facade

Jehangir S. Pocha, "Westerners Protest Beijing-Tibet Rail: Exiles Fear It Will Lead to Firmer Grip by China," *Boston Globe*, July 1, 2006. Reproduced by permission.

Tibetan exiles burn a Chinese flag after scaling the wall of the Chinese embassy in New Delhi, India, to protest the expansion of the Chinese railway into Tibet in 2006. © Desmond Boylan/ X00037/Reuters/Corbis.

of the central train station yesterday and unfurled a banner that read "China's Tibet Railway: Designed to Destroy."

Within minutes, security officers detained the trio, pulled down the banner, and bundled the activists out of sight as curious travelers watched.

The London-based Free Tibet Campaign identified the protesters as Kathy Ni Keefe, 36, of Sante Fe, N.M.; Katie Mallin, 34, of Britain; and Omi Hodwitz, a 29-year-old Canadian. They were released after three hours.

Earlier, in India, dozens of Tibetan exiles protesting the railway scaled the fence of the Chinese Embassy in New Delhi and set fire to Chinese flags before being arrested by local police.

The protests highlighted concerns among the activists and among Tibetan exiles that China will use the 710-mile-long railway, which is opening today [July 1, 2006], to consolidate its grip over Tibet.

Kate Woznow, a spokeswoman for the Free Tibet Campaign, said all the Beijing protesters were foreigners because of the risks for Tibetans to speak out in China and in Tibet. "We wanted to send a message globally that Tibetans are opposed to the launch of the Chinese-Tibetan railway," she said.

The $4.2 billion rail line will directly connect the Tibetan capital, Lhasa, with Beijing, 2,500 miles east, for the first time. The government said it will help promote economic growth in Tibet, one [of] the poorest regions in Asia.

Economic Development vs. Cultural Imperialism

But Tibetan exiles say China, which invaded and occupied Tibet in 1959, will use the railway to flood Tibet with Han Chinese, the main ethnic group of China.

Nawang Rapgyal, a spokesman for the Tibetan government-in-exile in India led by the Dalai Lama, said: "If [the railway] is used for political use—that is, the transfer of Chinese from China to Tibet—then it would be against the Tibetan people's wish and we will be protesting that."

The railway controversy erupted as the Chinese government and representatives of the Dalai Lama, the spiritual and political leader of Tibetans, are believed to be engaged in secret negotiations over the future of Tibet. To woo Beijing, the Dalai Lama has said he would drop Tibet's demand for independence from China in return for genuine autonomy.

But such a prospect angers many hard-line Tibetans, who have formed new organizations, such as the Tibetan Youth Congress, which operates in Dharamsala, northern India, to press their cause.

"Tibetans, deep in their hearts, know these negotiations will not serve any purpose," Kalsang Phuntsok Godrukpa, president of the Tibetan Youth Congress, said in a telephone interview.

"The negotiations are really a Chinese postponement policy, which will keep Tibetans engrossed and let Beijing tell the world that they are engaging Tibetans. But meanwhile, the Chinese will continue doing whatever they want to do, which is to completely steamroll the Tibetan people."

Godrukpa has been advocating more "direct action" against China, and Tibetan Youth Congress activists have been responsible for stirring up anti-Chinese protests in many countries the past few years. Beijing has launched a public relations blitz to counter criticism of the new railway.

The state-controlled media has celebrated the engineering prowess that went into building the newest and most significant part of the Tibet line, which connects Lhasa to Golmud in central Qinghai Province, 695 miles north. The train uses high-tech systems to keep stable in icy conditions, and its cabins are oxygenated to help passengers cope with Himalayan altitudes.

The Chinese government also is touting the Qinghai-Tibet line as a tourist attraction that will give passengers breathtaking views of Tibet's soaring mountains and azure skies.

Yet, it's hard to hide the tight control China exerts over Tibet. The province is closed to the international media. Rights groups say monks who profess allegiance to the Dalai Lama often are tortured, and the exploitation of the area's natural resources has gutted vast swaths of Tibet's once-pristine landscape.

Most Tibetans believe that the most potent threat to their existence would come from the massive migration of Han Chinese into Tibet.

Samdhong Rinpoche, prime minister of the Tibetan government-in-exile, estimates that Tibet has 2.3 million Tibetans, but 7 million Han Chinese—more than 100 times the number China officially gives.

"Tibetans in Tibet are turning into a minority," Rapgyal said.

Tibetans Stage Protests in the Months Before the 2008 Olympic Games in Beijing

USA Today

In the following viewpoint, a reporter examines the protests staged by Tibetans and their supporters in the months before the 2008 Summer Olympics in Beijing, China's capital. The Chinese saw the Olympics, says the viewpoint, both as confirmation that their nation had achieved great-power status and as a showcase for China's economic and technological achievements. But many Tibetans, both in Tibet itself and other regions of China, saw their own opportunity. According to USA Today, *they used the occasion to stage demonstrations in hopes of bringing greater worldwide attention to the Tibetan cause. Supported by the exiled Dalai Lama, Tibetans complained that China was systematically dismantling Tibet's unique culture through such means as sending Han (mainstream Chinese) residents to the region as well as the marginalization of Tibetan Buddhism. As the author of the viewpoint notes, the widespread protests were decisively quashed by Chinese authorities, who went so far as to ban foreign observers from certain areas and, allegedly, engage in widespread violence.*

When riot police with bulletproof shields lined up outside the monastery in this Qinghai province city [Amdo

Labrang] on Sunday [March 16, 2008], scared residents ducked indoors and wary businesses shut down.

But dozens of Tibetan monks marched up a hill outside Rongwo Monastery in defiance of an order to stay in their home. They set off fireworks and burned incense in a show of bravado as truckloads of paramilitary troops and plainclothes police officers surrounded the area.

Protests both big and small spread from Tibet into Qinghai and two other neighboring provinces Sunday as Tibetans defied a Chinese government crackdown and the Dalai Lama decried what he called the "cultural genocide" taking place in his homeland.

The demonstrations in Qinghai, Sichuan and Gansu provinces forced authorities to mobilize security forces across a broad expanse of western China.

In a sign that authorities were preparing for trouble, Associated Press and other foreign journalists were ordered out of the Tibetan parts of Gansu and Qinghai provinces by police who told them it was for their "safety."

Tibetans protest against Chinese rule in the Bakhor Square in Lhasa in March 2008, in the months leading up to the Olympic Games in Beijing. © AP Images/Andreas Steinbichler.

Meanwhile, police in the Tibetan capital, Lhasa, searched buildings as a Monday deadline loomed for people who took part in a violent anti-Chinese uprising last week to surrender or face severe punishment.

Tibet's governor Champa Phuntsok said Monday that 16 people died and dozens were wounded in the violence, which broke out in Lhasa on Friday. He described 13 of the dead as "innocent civilians," and said another three people died jumping out of buildings to avoid arrest. China's state media said earlier that 10 civilians were killed.

Speaking from India, the Dalai Lama, the spiritual leader of Tibetans, called for an international investigation into China's crackdown on demonstrators in Lhasa, which his exiled government claims left 80 people dead. China's state media has said 10 civilians were killed.

A Strong Accusation

"Whether intentionally or unintentionally, some kind of cultural genocide is taking place," the Dalai Lama said, referring to an influx of Chinese migration into Tibetan areas and restrictions on Buddhist practices—policies that have generated deep resentment among Tibetans.

Tensions also boiled over outside the county seat of Aba in Sichuan province when armed police tried to stop Tibetan monks from protesting, according to a witness who refused to give his name.

The witness said a policeman had been killed and three or four police vans had been set on fire. Eight bodies were brought to a nearby monastery while others reported that up to 30 protesters had been shot, according to activist groups the Tibetan Center for Human Rights and Democracy and the London-based Free Tibet Campaign. The claims could not be confirmed.

Sunday's demonstrations follow nearly a week of protests in Lhasa that escalated into violence Friday, with Tibetans attacking

Chinese and torching their shops, in the longest and fiercest challenge to Chinese rule in nearly two decades.

Complicating Beijing's task, the spreading protests fall two weeks before China's celebrations for the Beijing Olympics kick off with the start of the torch relay, which will pass through Tibet.

Though many were small in scale, the widening Tibetan protests are forcing Beijing to pursue suppression from town to town and province to province across its vast western region. Sunday's lockdown in Tongren required police imported from other towns, the locals said.

The Chinese government attempted to control what the public saw and heard about protests that erupted Friday. Access to YouTube.com, usually readily available in China, was blocked after videos appeared on the site Saturday showing foreign news reports about the Lhasa demonstrations, montages of photos, and scenes from Tibet-related protests abroad.

Restricting Information

Television news reports by CNN and the BBC were periodically cut during the day, and the screens went black during a live speech by the Dalai Lama carried on the networks.

China's communist government had hoped Beijing's hosting of the Aug. 8–24 Olympics would boost its popularity at home as well as its image abroad. Instead the event already has attracted the scrutiny of China's human rights record.

Thubten Samphel, a spokesman for the Dalai Lama's government, said multiple people inside Tibet had counted at least 80 corpses since the violence broke out Friday. He did not know how many of the bodies were protesters. The figures could not be independently verified because China restricts foreign media access to Tibet.

In Lhasa, hundreds of armed police and soldiers patrolled the streets on Sunday. Hong Kong Cable TV reported some 200 military vehicles, carrying 40 to 60 armed soldiers each, drove into the city center.

The 2008 Summer Olympics

The 2008 Summer Olympic Games were held in Beijing, the capital of the People's Republic of China. This was the first time the Olympics took place in China, and the event came to be considered a sign that China had become a true global power after many decades of chaos, instability, and international suspicion over the nature of China's communist regime.

Olympic officials chose Beijing as the 2008 host city in 2001 after having rejected earlier bids. They now considered China advanced enough economically to be able to build and maintain the sports venues that the Olympics would require as well as other facilities, such as the International Olympic Village for athletes. They took into account China's human rights and environmental records. But officials also recognized China's new status as a major economic power, a status it had achieved only since economic reforms took hold in the 1980s.

The Chinese built or renovated dozens of venues for the games, most notably the Beijing National Stadium, or "Bird's Nest." They also improved railroad and airport facilities, local transportation, and other aspects of the city's infrastructure for the many thousands of athletes, dignitaries, reporters, and other visitors who would be coming from around the world. These visitors and other observers ultimately deemed the Beijing Games a success largely unmarred by major problems or controversies. Among the athletic stars who emerged were US swimmer Michael Phelps and Jamaican sprinter Usain Bolt.

Not all in China were pleased with the Beijing Olympics. Tibetan advocates as well as representatives of other ethnic minorities took the opportunity to draw attention to their causes by staging protests. Allegedly, some of these protests were violently crushed by state forces. The Chinese government was also accused of stifling the spread of information by restricting the access of journalists to areas of protest or by closing down the Internet in affected areas. Protesters and their supporters in other countries hoped that, despite any Olympic triumphs, the world might pay attention to what they saw as the Chinese government's continued violation of basic human rights.

Footage showed the streets were mostly empty other than the security forces. Messages on loudspeakers warned residents to "discern between enemies and friends, maintain order" and "have a clear stand to oppose violence, maintain stability."

James Miles, a BBC correspondent in Lhasa, said troops carrying automatic rifles were "letting off the occasional shot." He said people were scared to come out of their homes for fear of being hit by a bullet.

Westerners who were told to leave Lhasa and arrived by plane in the city of Chengdu said they heard gunshots and explosions throughout Saturday and overnight.

"The worst day was yesterday. It was completely chaotic. There was running and screaming in the street," said Gerald Scott Flint, director of the medical aid group Volunteer Medics Worldwide, who had been in Lhasa four days. Flint said he could see fires burning six or more blocks away.

Tashi Wangdi, president of the Office of Tibet that represents the Dalai Lama in New York, called the departure of tourists worrisome.

"I think there will be total blackout of information to the outside world," he said. "Our worry is they will be more brutal and will use more force now."

The unrest in Tibet began March 10 on the anniversary of a 1959 uprising against Chinese rule of the region. Tibet was effectively independent for decades before communist troops entered in 1950.

The Tibetan communities living far outside what China calls modern Tibet are parts of former provinces of past Tibetan kingdoms, and many inhabitants still revere the Dalai Lama.

"We want freedom. We want the Dalai Lama to come back to this land," said a monk from Rongwo in Tongren. The monks display his pictures, though they have been ordered to remove them.

Inspired by the protests in Lhasa, monks and Tibetans in the town of Xiahe in Gansu province staged two days of protests, one peaceful in which they raised Tibetan national flags, the other in which government offices were smashed and police tear-gassed the crowd of more than 1,000.

Authorities clamped a curfew on Xiahe overnight. Patrols of riot police, in black uniforms, helmets and flak jackets, and armed police in green uniforms carrying batons marched through the town Sunday in groups of 10 and 20.

Smaller protests were reported in two other nearby towns, witnesses said, in both cases drawing truckloads of armed police.

In the Gansu provincial capital of Lanzhou, more than 100 Tibetan students staged a sit-down protest on a playing field at Northwest Minorities University, according to the activist group Free Tibet.

China: Tibetan Monasteries Placed Under Direct Rule

Human Rights Watch

Since completing its takeover of Tibet in 1951, China has called the area the Tibetan Autonomous Region, attempting to govern it with the assistance of Tibetans who have demonstrated their loyalty to China. In the following viewpoint, writers for the humanitarian organization Human Rights Watch report on an important change in that general approach. This change places Chinese government officials in direct charge of Tibet's most characteristic of institutions: Buddhist monasteries. Rather than the monasteries being managed by religious experts who maintain high status among Tibetans, they will be continually observed by cadres, or Chinese government officials. The Chinese, according to the viewpoint, claim that such a move is necessary to prevent the monasteries from becoming the source of protests or separatist movements. But the authors also cite observers who suggest that the move is a major threat to any supposed Tibetan autonomy, or freedom, and that a number of Tibetan monks have already killed themselves in protest.

New York—The Chinese government has ended a key policy of allowing Tibetan monasteries to be run by monks who comply with government regulations and have instead introduced a system that will place almost every monastery in Tibet under the direct rule of government officials who will be permanently stationed in each religious institution, Human Rights Watch said today.

On January 4, 2012, the Party Secretary of the Tibetan Autonomous Region (TAR), Chen Quanguo, announced that government or party officials will be stationed in almost all monasteries permanently, and that in some cases they will have the senior rank and pay of a deputy director of a provincial-level government department. The permanent posting of government or party officials inside monasteries is unprecedented in Tibet, let alone at such a senior level.

"Although the Chinese government has placed many restrictions on the practice of religion in Tibet, these new regulations represent an entirely new level of intervention by the state," said Sophie Richardson, China director at Human Rights Watch. "This measure, coupled with the increasing presence of government workers within monasteries, will surely exacerbate tensions in the region."

According to official documents, the new policy, known as the "Complete Long-term Management Mechanism for Tibetan Buddhist Monasteries," is described as, "critical for taking the initiative in the struggle against separatism," and aims to "ensure that monks and nuns do not take part in activities of splitting up the motherland and disturbing social order."

The order to post resident cadres within monasteries in the TAR was contained in an "important memorandum" on "mechanisms to build long-term stability in Tibet" issued by Politburo Standing Committee Member Jia Qinglin, Minister of Public Security Meng Jianzhu and other state leaders in late December 2011. That memorandum orders the TAR to "have cadres stationed in the main monasteries to further strengthen and innovate monastery management," according to an official news report on December 20.

"This new decision is a major departure. It overturns the central guarantee of 'autonomy' that has guided policy on Tibet for decades," said Richardson.

China's policy for Tibetan monasteries, first introduced in 1962, provides that all monasteries are supposed to be run by monks—under close governmental supervision, but with only indirect involvement of officials. The policy was abandoned during the Cultural Revolution (from 1966 to 1979 in Tibet), when almost all monasteries were closed and many were physically destroyed.

The policy allowing nominal self-rule of monasteries was reinstated in the early 1980s and had been upheld ever since. China's constitution guarantees freedom of religious belief, but control over religious activities of ethnic minority groups such as Tibetans and Uighurs has always been markedly more severe.

Under the previous policy, all places of worship, including Tibetan monasteries, have until now been administered by a structure called the "Democratic Management Committee." Although the nomination and selection of the committee members are controlled by government and party officials (and rigid political constraints are imposed on the nominees), the committees were comprised of monks who had at least been elected by their own community.

The new system now requires an unelected "Management Committee"—also referred to as *zhusi danwei/gongzuozu* ("monastic government work-unit")—to be established in every monastery, with up to 30 lay officials stationed in each monastery, depending on the size of the institution, according to a February 15, 2012 article in the government-run *Global Times*. The new "Management Committees" will run the monasteries and will have authority over the previous "Democratic Management Committees," which will now be responsible for rituals and other matters.

The new arrangement is referred to as "the combination of management by administration with self-rule" in monasteries and means that "officials are selected and sent to manage the monastery together with the monks." In monasteries that are at "grassroots level," the administration will be in the hands of officials from the local village-level organizations of the government or party.

The new system of cadre-supervised monasteries is the result of a research project initiated in 2008 by the United Front Work Department, the agency of the CCP in charge of religion and nationality issues. The research was initiated as an "emergency response project" by a team of experts in Beijing following widespread unrest in Tibetan areas in 2008, according to an August 26, 2011 article by Gong Xuezeng, a professor at China's Central Party School.

In November 2011, the authorities began establishing the "Management Committees" in the 1,787 monasteries that are allowed to operate in the TAR. The stated objectives of the new management scheme are:

- "to promote lasting political stability in the TAR and other Tibetan areas,"
- to "establish harmonious monasteries," and
- to ensure that "monks and nuns have the freedom to perform their religious rituals."

However, according to Gong's article, the temples will have to "rectify their religious style," though the meaning of this is unclear.

The rationale for the new system is explained in official documents as "enhancing social management" in temples. This is seen as developing an underlying objective established in 1994 which aimed to "adapt Tibetan Buddhism to socialism." The new theory argues that since monks are members of society as well as monks, their institutions should be run by social forces, meaning party and government organizations. As a result, in the new system, besides the party cadres stationed within monasteries, numerous local government offices at each level will have day-to-day responsibility for directly managing different aspects of Tibetan monastic life. Twenty-four government organs, including the offices of public security, foreign affairs, and justice, are listed in regulations issued in Aba (*Ngaba* in Tibetan) prefecture in 2009 as involved in managing local monasteries (article 4).

Under the new system, according to Gong's article, these government offices are also required to provide practical services, such as running water, electricity, roads, and social security payments, to monks and monasteries, "especially those that are supportive and helpful for patriotism."

In eastern Tibetan areas outside the TAR, reports indicate that instead of establishing a new committee, the old Democratic Management Committees will be retained as the leading body in each monastery, but are expected to have a government official inserted as the deputy director of each committee. For example, regulations have been passed in Qinghai, which place each township-level monastery in that province under a "Masses Supervision and Appraisal Committee" that will supervise, monitor, and report to the government on the management and religious practices in local monasteries.

Two leading monasteries in the TAR, Tashilhunpo (*Zhashilunbu* in Chinese) in Shigatse (*Xigaze* in Chinese) and Champaling (*Qiangbaling* in Chinese) in Chamdo (*Changdu* in Chinese), will be allowed to retain their Democratic Management Committees without creating a committee of unelected officials above it because they have "have actively explored the path of self-education and self-rule, creating an effective management pattern with their own characteristics" and so have "achieved monastery self-rule and democratic management." The two monasteries are considered politically reliable and are the traditional seats of two lamas, the Panchen Lama and Phagpa-lha Gelek Namgyal (a leading lama), who hold national-level office in China.

Human Rights Watch called the decision to impose direct rule on almost all monasteries and to station cadres permanently in them is a worrying indication that the state is becoming increasingly invasive in its management of religion in Tibet. These policies are likely to lead to further tensions and to further exacerbate social difficulties that have been growing in Tibetan areas since 2008. The move also appears to undermine statements by China's Premier, Wen Jiabao, this week that "we should respect Tibetan compatriots' freedom of religious belief" and that "we must treat all of our Tibetan compatriots with equality and respect."

Strict security measures and restrictions on fundamental freedoms in Tibetan areas were imposed, following a series of street protests against Chinese rule in March 2008. Immediately following the protests, thousands of people were detained and arrested, though the total number is unknown, and at least two Tibetans were executed in October 2009 on charges stemming from their involvement in the protests. Security measures and restrictions on the exercise of religious freedom imposed on monasteries in Aba (Tibetan: Ngaba) and Ganzi (Tibetan: Kardze) Tibetan autonomous prefectures in Sichuan were especially severe, including intimidating raids and arbitrary detentions of monks, as detailed by Human Rights Watch.

Twenty-eight Tibetans have set themselves on fire since March 2011 to protest China's policies, including at least 18 from Aba.

"If the Chinese government is committed to reducing tensions in Tibetan areas, it should repeal these policies immediately," said Richardson.

The Tibetan Government-in-Exile Marks a Sad Anniversary

Tibetan Parliament in Exile

The following viewpoint consists of an official statement made by Tibet's government-in-exile on the fifty-third anniversary of what it refers to as Tibetan National Uprising Day. This unsuccessful rebellion in 1959 led ultimately to the exile of the Dalai Lama and other Tibetan leaders and the establishment of the government-in-exile in Dharamsala, India. Leaders used this 2012 commemoration as an occasion to remind the world of their grievances against the Chinese government, from abuse of the land, to the repression of Tibetan Buddhism, to the importation of ethnic Han Chinese into the region. The viewpoint also notes that, especially since a series of demonstrations in 2008, Chinese reprisals against Tibetan resistance have been particularly harsh; some Tibetans have resorted to the gesture of self-immolation, or burning themselves to death. Tibet's leaders also try to remind China, and the world, that the two peoples have for centuries been neighbors, not citizens of a single nation-state.

The 53rd anniversary of the 1959 10th March Tibetan National Uprising is being commemorated under the dark shadows of 25 Tibetans driven to self-immolation, out of which 19 have succumbed to their injuries and 8 others became victim of the indiscriminate police firings on peaceful Tibetan demonstrators in Tibet in the last one year alone [March 2011–March 2012]. The whereabouts and well-being of others are unknown. Many have been incarcerated and many other forced disappearance cases have been reported. Even as we meet here today, we can well imagine what might be going on inside Tibet now.[1]

In fact, since the 2008 nationwide demonstrations, the situation in Tibet has continued to be tense. Farmers' non-cooperation in farming in 2009 and student's protests against the imposition of Mandarin [Chinese] language in 2010 are among many other peaceful protests and demonstrations that continued to the present day. Monk Tapey was the first to resort to this action when he self immolated on 27th of February 2009.

On behalf of all the Tibetans, the Tibetan Parliament in Exile pays homage to those who lost their lives and pray for their noble rebirth. To those who continue to suffer, we share your pain. Now we all have to put our efforts together to make sure that their sacrifices do not go in vain.

Why do the peaceful Tibetans have to undergo so much pain? For the freedom to think, to express, to act and of choice, just as anyone in the free world enjoys. That is an individual's birthright. Burning one's body in full consciousness and with conviction involves thorough deliberation with the self, conviction and mental courage, especially when one is motivated by benefit for others through self-sacrifice. Under other circumstances, the tendency is normally to hurt the other. That is not the case in Tibet. Premier Wen Jiabao in his effort to hide the reality of the situation and to divert the attention of the Chinese and the international community has deplorably termed the self immolations in Tibet as an act of terrorism. We would not be surprised if they adopt this view into law tomorrow!

Hundreds and thousands of protests take place in China, but when it comes to managing protest demonstrations, it is teargas on Chinese and bullets on Tibetans. Will there ever be a respite for the peaceful Tibetans, who just long for the return of His Holiness the Dalai Lama and freedom. How many more Tibetan lives have to be lost till an amicable solution is found or will the whole of Tibet fall victim to the ongoing cultural genocide?

All human beings, irrespective of differences in gender, race, color, wealth and political ideology aspire for happiness. To freely practice and promote your language, religion, culture and way of life are fundamental to human happiness. Unfortunately, in the present day China, there are not enough sensible leaders who understand that one's happiness lies in the happiness of others in this interdependent world. Turning a deaf ear and blind eye to the reality of the situation will have serious consequences. When a time comes regretting what could have been done would be too late.

Neighbors, Not Subjects

Since time immemorial, Tibetans and the Chinese lived as any two good neighbors could be. Tibetans have neither harmed the Chinese people nor interest of China. We enjoyed relatively good spiritual relations with all the emperors of China—be it the Mongol Yuan, Chinese Ming or Manchu Ching dynasties. None of our neighboring countries have directly interfered in the administration of Tibet. Only when the wave of communism swept over Russia and China, Tibet too fell victim to Mao's [Zedong's] voracious expansionist appetite.

Considering the reality of the situation in Tibet and what we are up against, His Holiness the Dalai Lama has taken a very pragmatic and mutually beneficial step by not seeking independence but meaningful autonomy for all the Tibetan areas—thereby, addressing the biggest concern of China—sovereignty. Post-devolution of His Holiness' responsibilities, we remain committed to the Middle Way Approach through non-violence and a lasting negotiated settlement. Nine rounds of dialogue have not yielded any tangible results, mainly due to the intransigence of the Chinese leaders, who feel that if they manage to curb the activities of His Holiness the Dalai Lama and the Tibetans in exile through diplomatic and political coercions, the Tibetans inside could be muzzled to subservience.

With no positive response from China, the dialogue remains disrupted, despite our all-out effort with the written proposal which they asked for, and explanations to their misrepresentations as per the provisions in the Constitution and the autonomy law enacted by the National People's Congress [NPC]. The essence of a law is not only in enacting it but in implementing it. To diffuse the urgency of the situation in Tibet and to seek a lasting solution to the issue of Tibet, in the interest of China and in the interest of the Tibetans, the Chinese leadership should immediately engage in serious negotiation with our leadership with the commitment and conviction to come to a mutually agreeable solution. We have no doubt that the resolution of the Tibet Issue in a just manner will have many positive effects on peace and stability of the whole geo-strategic region.

In the ongoing NPC and CPPCC [Chinese People's Consultative Political Conference], Mr. Jia Qinglin, President of the NPCC made baseless allegations against His Holiness the Dalai Lama for instigating unrest in Tibet that is laughable. The whole world knows what His Holiness stands for. The functioning of the Central Tibetan Administration is transparent and we have time and again offered our offices for scrutiny to the Chinese authorities.

Meanwhile in Tibet, the policies and programs of the Chinese authorities have always been aimed at eradication of the Tibetan national identity. They have successfully done that with the Manchus, and it is happening right now in [ethnic-minority regions] Inner Mongolia, Tibet and Uighur.

Turning Tibetans into Second-Class Citizens

Much of what Tibet was has been destroyed in the last more than 60 years. Through planned demographic aggression by way of infrastructure development, unscrupulous exploitation of natural resources and urbanization; cities and towns in Tibet have been taken over by the majority Chinese population. New migrant mining townships are sprouting all over. Tibetans are marginalized politically, economically and socially. It will not be long before Tibet towns become small pockets of Tibetan residents in a Chinese over-populated Tibet. A party ideologue and United Work Front's Vice Minister, Zhu Weiqun's recent posturing in a party journal on doing away with ethnic identities to promote nationalism sounds ominous—like fixing the last nail on the coffin.

When your jobs are being snatched away by others, opportunities taken away, considered second-class citizens in your own land, how would one feel? Whereas [mainstream] Han Chinese receive preferential treatment for a posting in Tibet—better pay, natural promotions, free education and government jobs for children etc. These discriminatory measures are difficult for the Tibetans to digest.

More than that, striking at the very heart and mind of the Tibetan people is the freedom to practice religion. Tibetans have been devout Buddhists, a belief embedded into its culture and way of life, acquired over more than 13 centuries. Due to which, Tibetans have lived in perfect harmony with nature and peaceful co-existence with our neighbors.

The unique culture of the Tibetans rooted in Buddha's teaching. Along with other religions, it has the potential for generating a more compassionate and a peaceful world. Even after more than 60 years the Chinese leaders have not learnt that the carrot and stick policy did not bring happiness for the Tibetan people. For 60 long years, the authorities tried to brainwash the Tibetans. Look at Tibet today. Tibetans in Tibet, particularly the younger generations, who have never seen His Holiness the Dalai Lama or those who were born after the Cultural Revolution are leading the movement inside Tibet.

Look at the reality. Some estimate [there are] about 13 million believers in the Communist Party! It is time the authorities grant religious freedom to all religious groups. Stop turning the study centers and places of worship into mere tourist attraction. How on earth will it help to create a harmonious society when [Chinese Communist leaders] Mao, Deng [Xiaoping], Jiang [Zemin] and Hu's pictures were displayed in the monasteries by force alongside statues of the Buddha when there is widespread unhappiness? How are you supposed to win over [a] people's mind and heart by turning the monasteries and nunneries into virtual military garrison or police posts, communist party offices? How would you feel, if your movements are restricted as well as monitored all the time, just as you are doing it to the monks and nuns? How would a believer feel, if the reincarnation of the high lamas have to be approved by an atheist government? Rubbing salt on the open wounds in the Tibetan hearts and minds will only breed more defiance. When there is no human dignity, there is nothing to lose.

Disrespect and Bad Government

Forcing the Tibetan nomads into settled communities in or around existing townships not only had adverse impact on environmental stewardship but also on the way of life and future livelihood of the displaced Tibetans. Managing the watershed area of the some of major rivers of Asia that flows into 10 neighboring countries including China requires modern scientific research as well as indigenous wisdom acquired over centuries of having lived in the region. Instead of pushing away the Tibetan nomads, the government should make the local Tibetans partners in regenerating programs. The authorities should not only review and stop the ongoing program but also provide full compensation and facilitate better livelihood for a smooth transition from the traditional way of life to a new way of life to the victims of the massive social engineering directed by the government.

No one questions the growth of China as a global power economically and militarily. Now, it has to grow into a responsible, trusted and respected global leader. However, neither can trust be built without proper understanding and respect for each other nor by use of force and intimidation. Without trust, there cannot be harmony and stability. Respect has to be earned. Harmony within the nation cannot be achieved till people are given freedom and, for instance, [a] harmonious neighborhood cannot be maintained by claiming the whole of South China Sea. For a start, China could release all the political prisoners including Panchen Rinpoche [a prominent lama] to build trust.

When we were younger, we were instilled the value of supporting the underdog, who is bullied. Today when China is bullying the Tibetans, Uighurs and their own people, the world community still courts the bully. We do of course understand that there are many more urgent problems like Syria, Iran, North Korea and much larger economic, energy, security and environmental issues. Having said that, I wish to stress that the self immolations in Tibet in large numbers is not such a small issue. The powerful nations of the world were very much part of the Tibetan history when we lost our country. Now we feel it is time for the world leaders to reiterate more forcefully on the need to settle the Tibet issue through dialogue. Since we are not asking for separation, that does not go against your One China policy and it addresses the main concern of China—its sovereignty.

Our struggle will continue. The UN [United Nations] should not be a pawn in the hands of the veto wielding few. We need all your support now! Though we have to find a solution by talking with China, the catalyst to make it happen sooner is in your hands, before it is too late. Let our people also share the freedom that the free world enjoys.

Hopes for a Better Future

As the World Bank said, China has reached a turning point. Just as it recommended, it is time for sweeping political and economic changes. Otherwise, today's economic boon could turn into China's bane tomorrow. China ending up [in] social and political chaos will have serious consequences on the world. It is time to change now! I am sure better sense will prevail over the Chinese leadership. We also hope that at this moment of China's turning point, the genuine and legitimate aspirations of the Tibetan people will also be addressed.

The Tibetan Parliament in Exile take this opportunity to thank the government and people for their unwavering support and the International Community who took the side of truth, non-violence, justice, freedom and human dignity.

To conclude, I again wish to express our gratitude to His Holiness the Dalai Lama for his guidance and leadership; pray for the reunion of all the Tibetans in Tibet and for the long life of His Holiness the Dalai Lama.

Note

1. In case of any possible discrepancy in meaning, the original Tibetan text should be treated as authoritative. (This note has been added.)

CHAPTER 2

Controversies Surrounding Tibet

Chapter Exercises

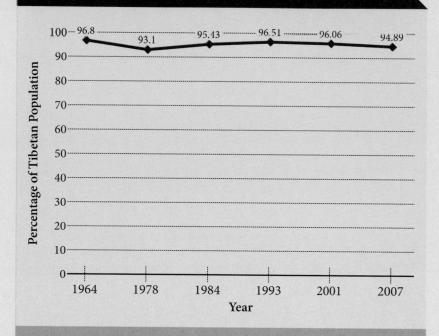

PERCENTAGE OF ETHNIC TIBETANS IN THE TOTAL POPULATION OF TIBET, 1964–2007

Percentage of Tibetan Population

96.8 · · · · · · · · · · · · · · · · · · 95.43 · · · · · · 96.51 · · · · · · · · 96.06 · · · · · · · · 94.89

93.1

Year: 1964 · 1978 · 1984 · 1993 · 2001 · 2007

Source: China Tibetology Research Center, "Report on the Economic and Social Development of Tibet," March 30, 2009.

1. Analyze the Chart

Question 1: What percentage of the population of Tibet was made up of ethnic Tibetans in 1964?

Question 2: What were the only years in which the population of ethnic Tibetans in Tibet went below 96 percent of the total?

Question 3: In what year was the ethnic Tibetan population at its lowest as a percentage of the total?

2. Writing Prompt

Take on the role of a newspaper editor or the editor of a major online news website. Write an editorial on the question of whether China's actions in Tibet, including alleged targeting of its religion, amount to a "cultural genocide."

3. Group Activity

Form groups and debate whether or not the interests of Hollywood actors and other celebrities help to increase awareness of Tibet or, instead, trivialize its culture and provide an inaccurate perspective.

Tibetan Dissident to Accuse Chinese of Torture and Genocide

Clifford Coonan

Many Tibetans who have gone into exile since the 1950 Chinese takeover have sought to bring what they see as injustices to the attention of the world. In the following viewpoint, journalist Clifford Coonan examines a civil suit in Spain's highest court against former Chinese leaders Jiang Zemin and Li Peng, whom Tibetans and their supporters accuse of various human rights abuses: the dilution and destruction of Tibetan culture and even genocide. Coonan focuses in particular on Tibetan activist Tenzin Tsundue, who provided testimony to the Spanish court. The Spanish high court ended the case in 2010 on the grounds that the alleged victims did not have direct enough links to Spain. Still, other legal complaints related to Tibet are pending in the country. Coonan is a Beijing-based correspondent for the UK's Independent newspaper.

Beijing, July 3—Tenzin Tsundue, a Tibetan poet and activist, takes his fight to Britain today when he files a sworn testimony detailing atrocities he says he saw and experienced while in prison in the remote Himalayan region.

Mr Tsundue's testimony is a stark litany of beatings and torture doled out during his imprisonment without trial in 1999, and will be submitted today to the Foreign and Commonwealth Office legalisation office, where it will be officially notarised.

The testimony is for a criminal suit filed in Spain's High Court by three Tibet support groups accusing former president Jiang Zemin and ex-parliament chief Li Peng, both of whom retired in 2003, of committing genocide and crimes against humanity in Tibet.

"Many European countries speak of peace and human rights and harmony. But on business they all cosy up to China, it's hypocritical. Through asking for justice in an international court I hope they will have second thoughts," Mr Tsundue said. "The Tibetan people should have the right to run their own country, not the Chinese people," he said.

The case accuses the retired leaders, who were in office during the 1980s and 1990s, of authorising massacres and torture in Tibet. The court could call for the Chinese government to arrest those accused of human rights abuse—and even impound their property.

Tibet has been under the control of China since 1950 when the People's Liberation Army marched into Tibet. Less than a decade later the Himalayan region's spiritual leader, the Dalai Lama, fled after a failed uprising. Tales of torture and abuse have abounded over the past four decades.

China has condemned the lawsuit, calling it absurd, and Beijing has accused Madrid of meddling in its affairs. Madrid is also investigating charges of genocide against the Falun Gong spiritual movement.

Emilie Hunter, a spokesperson for the Madrid-based Friends of Tibet Committee, said she hoped that the effect of filing the testimony in Britain would be to stimulate broader government and public interest in the issue.

The lawsuit coincides with the opening of a hi-tech train line between Beijing and Lhasa, which the Chinese say will give Tibet

Tenzin Tsundue is restrained by Indian security personnel during a staged protest of China prime minister Wen Jiabao's visit to the Indian Institute of Science in Bangalore in 2005.
© Dibyangshu Sarkar/AFP/Getty Images.

an economic boost, but which Tibetan activists fear will lead to a dilution of Tibetan culture.

"This is one way to fight Beijing—they may not listen to us Tibetans but this is a way to speak to Beijing non-violently with law and show this is injustice and we want them to address this," Mr Tsundue said.

The activist lives, along with approximately 110,000 other Tibetans including the Dalai Lama, in Dharamsala, close to the border with India. He was arrested in 1999 while crossing into Tibet at Ladakh and held for three months in two prisons. Here he says he experienced, and witnessed, the treatment of Tibetans who had been jailed for "counter-revolutionary" crimes.

"Over three months I was beaten, starved, became infested with lice and had a red-hot poker brandished in front of my eyes. For me, those long sessions of interrogation were so intimidating, humiliating, and disturbing that many times I found myself crying in the middle of night in my dark prison cell," he said.

He said he fears for the life of one political prisoner, Dawa Gyaltsen, who was arrested in 1996 and sentenced to 18 years in prison for designing and distributing "free Tibet" posters. He is now being held in Lhasa's notorious Drapchi prison.

Mr Tsundue's views are more extreme than those of the Dalai Lama, whom the Chinese view as a dangerous separatist who wants to wrest control of Tibet away from China. Beijing accuses him of continuing to spark independence movements among the 2.7 million Tibetans and refuses to allow him back inside its borders.

For his part, the Dalai Lama, who won the Nobel Peace Prize in 1989, insists he is a moderate who preaches a "middle way", which seeks special autonomy for Tibet within China, not independence.

Many Tibetans, include Mr Tsundue, remain fiercely loyal to the figure they regard as a god-king. "For us Tibetans the Dalai Lama is our leader and he is our Buddha," Mr Tsundue said. "He has an immense sense of compassion and forgiveness. I don't have the power of the Buddha to compromise on independence.

"On the political front I ask for independence for Tibet. The Tibetan people should have the right to run their own country and not China," he said.

Tsundue's Testimony

My name is Tenzin Tsundue. I am a Tibetan born and brought up in India. On 4 March 1997, I walked across the India-Tibet border. I was apprehended at Cha-gang by border police. For eight days I was interrogated every morning for many hours and throughout these interrogation sessions, they kept asking me who sent me, who backed me in my mission, what was it about, who I was meeting in Tibet . . . the interrogators, who were mostly Tibetans, would kick me, punch me in the chest and often slapped my face . . . Sometimes, after a hard slap I would almost go deaf, and for a long time I remained dazed. These sessions of interrogation were very intimidating, humiliating and mentally so traumatising that sometimes in the middle of the night in my cell, I found myself crying . . . I was never produced before any court nor given any opportunity for legal support. In the jail, the food was poor and served only twice a day, leaving us starved all the time.

In Tibet, Defiant Self-Immolations Spread Beyond Monks, Nuns

Robert Marquand

In the following viewpoint, a US newspaper reports on self-immolations by Tibetans in protest against Chinese policies toward Tibet. At the time of writing, self-immolation protests had risen to forty-five, mostly by Buddhist monks and nuns in protest against Chinese policies and actions directed toward their faith and identity. The most recent self-immolation took the life of a lay woman who called out for the return of the Tibetan spiritual leader, the Dalai Lama, and for freedom for Tibet. Although the Dalai Lama protests against this kind of action, religious leaders in Tibet feel that the people are in a life and death struggle for their faith and identity. The self-immolation of lay people may indicate that a tipping-point in opposition to Chinese policies has been reached. Robert Marquand is a staff writer for the Christian Science Monitor.

Yesterday, a Tibetan mother died after her self-immolation in protest of the Dalai Lama's exile and the lack of freedom in Tibet. The number of self-immolators has risen to 45 in the past 1½ years.

While Chinese Olympic gold medals in London make headlines, far away, on the Himalayan roof of the world, two more young Tibetans—a mother and a monk—set themselves on fire in protest of Chinese policies on Tibet, including the lack of return of the Dalai Lama, the exiled spiritual leader.

The two "self-immolations" raise to 45 the number of Tibetans setting themselves alight, most since March of 2011. The immolations started with Buddhist monks and nuns who see themselves in an increasingly desperate struggle for the ancient land and its people, and who say their Tibetan identity and faith is being stamped out by aggressive Chinese policies and actions.

Yet 13 of the self-immolations in Tibet this year suggest that ordinary Tibetans are starting to torch themselves, and that the cases appear to be spreading geographically and are less confined to a few dissident monasteries.

"The self-immolations have now jumped a number of fences. There are more of them and they are more diverse," says Steven Marshall, a member of the Congressional-Executive Commission on China in Washington, who had extensive experience in Tibet in the 1980s and 1990s. "We are seeing immolations in the lay community, not only among monks and nuns where it started. It is also spreading into a greater area, not just the [Tibet Autonomous Region], but Qinghai and Gansu [provinces abutting the Tibet Autonomous Region]."

Yesterday, a mother of two, Dolkar Tso, from a farming family, set herself alight at a monastery in Gansu Province, which abuts the Tibetan Autonomous Region. She died from the flames. The International Campaign for Tibet in London cited exile sources in a statement saying she called out for the return of the Dalai Lama and for freedom in Tibet, following a pattern in other cases.

On Monday, a young monk from the Kirti monastery, 21-year-old Lobsang Tsultrim, set himself on fire in the region of Ngaba in Sichuan Province. Exile reports say he was still alive when taken away by a police car. Lobsang is the 27th monk from the Ngaba area to self-immolate, and the eighth from the Kirti monastery. His act took place on a street that is alternately being called "Martyrs Road" or "Heroes Road."

Dalai Lama Opposed Self-Immolation

While the Dalai Lama has consistently opposed self-immolations as a violation on the sacredness of life, Tibetans are continuing to do it in an act seen as indicative of the depth of feeling and desperation. Self-immolations are new and not part of any previous Tibetan protest tradition.

Tibetan Buddhist leaders have described the mood inside Tibet as a life and death struggle for the future of their faith and identity, and say that time is running out.

"They are calling for Dalai Lama's return because they are in this very serious moment, very serious, in which the Tibetan nation, identity, culture, the spiritual tradition, are all being closed down by Chinese aggression," says Kate Saunders, the spokeswoman for International Campaign for Tibet in London. "There is a very powerful feeling that time is running out, and that the connection between the people and what the Dalai Lama represents is being broken. These young people are sacrificing out of desperation that this spiritual connection not be broken. What they are calling out as they burn is for the return of the Dalai Lama, and for freedom in Tibet."

A year ago today, the Dalai Lama stepped down as official head of the government in exile after decades, but retains preeminence as the spiritual leader of Tibetans. In Tibetan monasteries, China continues to oversee aspects of religious instruction, control the appointment of teachers, give patriotic loyalty tests—actions that many Tibetans protest as serious infringements by Beijing on the faith.

Photos of the Dalai Lama in Tibet are forbidden.

"All monasteries must display pictures of Mao Zedong and Chinese President Hu Jintao and fly the Chinese flag. In numerous monasteries, forced patriotic reeducation campaigns are

Tibetan Buddhism

Born in India some 2,500 years ago, the Buddhist religion spread northward into Tibet between A.D. 700 and 1200. The Tibetan form of the religion combines features of the major branches of Mahayana and Theravada Buddhism with elements of earlier pre-Buddhist rituals and even aspects of Hinduism. Often described as a Tantric form of Buddhism, the Tibetan faith preaches that it is possible for some people to achieve full enlightenment in this lifetime. Those who do so are considered living Buddhas, or bodhisattvas, figures who help others achieve enlightenment. Meanwhile, for most believers, following Buddhist teachings is more a way of life than a set of religious practices and beliefs.

Meditation is central to Tibetan Buddhism. Many believers spend part or even all of their lives as monks and nuns, and until China began its transformation of the area, Tibet was dotted with thousands of monasteries. Through meditation believers hope to

under way," states Lobsang Sangay, who now heads a newly democratic government in exile in Dharamsala, India, in a statement this week. "Monks or nuns refusing to cooperate with Chinese policies are evicted from monasteries or arrested," and in some cases nuns have been asked to stomp on the images of the Dalai Lama.

Some Tibetan experts say the past year of self-immolations represent a "tipping point" in the deepening clashes between locals and Chinese authorities. But a consensus is also developing that Tibetan anger and discontent is near full boil. Tibetan nationalism is on the rise, seen partly through videos capturing enormous crowds attending the funeral services of the immolators.

"We are past a tipping point . . . the situation has already tipped," argues Mr. Marshall. "If lay Tibetans are now more awaken the spiritual force that lies within them. They might describe the moment when this happens as being struck by a thunderbolt thrown by the original Buddha, the Adi-Buddha, who is the source of all subsequent enlightenment. Sessions of meditation often involve the use of sacred chants and prayers.

Rituals and sacred objects are very important in Tibetan Buddhism as well. These objects include mandalas, which are circular designs thought to represent the universe. In certain rituals, Buddhas and bodhisattvas are "placed" on the mandala, giving believers the opportunity to establish contact with them. Some Tibetans use mandalas to fend off evil spirits and demons—beliefs that largely originate from pre-Buddhist traditions.

The prayer wheel is another important ritual object. Some of these wheels are large and fixed permanently inside monasteries. Others are small enough to be carried by believers on ritual pilgrimages. Either way, they hold prayers, chants, or other sacred statements that can be rotated around a central axis. Keeping the prayer wheel in constant rotation is among the clearest acts of devotion in Tibetan Buddhism.

prone to express less hope for the future, that is a problem for the [Chinese Communist] Party."

Beijing authorities often equate support for the Dalai Lama as synonymous with "succession." In recent months, they have vastly ramped up security forces in Tibet armed with fire extinguishers and "hooks" used to collar those who are trying to self-immolate. There is also a new and sophisticated Chinese media campaign. A multilingual, state-run CCTV series of broadcasts this summer on "The Dalai Clique and the Self-Immolation Events" essentially accuses the leader and other Buddhists of promoting the self-burnings, and includes on-the-ground graphic video footage and interviews with local Chinese police chiefs.

The region, meanwhile, is shut off from most foreign and Western journalists, NGOs, and human rights groups.

China's 100 Million Religious Believers Must Banish Their "Superstitions," Says Official

Ben Blanchard

In the following viewpoint, a British journalist reports on the ambivalent state approach to religion in China. China is officially atheist and Marxist, according to the State Administration of Religious Affairs in China, and wants people to deal with life issues in ways based on science, but it recognizes that it takes a long time to change long-held beliefs and that religion could be a force for good. In addition, the Chinese government has taken a more relaxed approach to religion in the last three decades after it began making economic reforms. The government has even tried to use religion to maintain social harmony and stability. However, the state continues to exercise tight control over Tibetans, Uighur Muslims, and Christians, and is wary of religion as a source of unrest. Ben Blanchard is a journalist who has written for The Independent and for Reuters.

China is struggling to get its estimated 100 million religious believers to banish superstitious beliefs about things like sickness and death, the country's top religious affairs official told a state-run newspaper.

Wang Zuoan, head of the State Administration of Religious Affairs, said there had been an explosion of religious belief in China along with the nation's economic boom, which he attributed to a desire for reassurance in an increasingly complex world.

While religion could be a force for good in officially atheist China, it was important to ensure people were not mislead, he told the Study Times, a newspaper published by the Central Party School which trains rising officials.

"For a ruling party which follows Marxism, we need to help people establish a correct world view and to scientifically deal with birth, ageing, sickness and death, as well as fortune and misfortune, via popularising scientific knowledge," he said, in rare public comments on the government's religious policy.

"But we must realise that this is a long process and we need to be patient and work hard to achieve it," Wang added in the latest issue of the Study Times, which reached subscribers on Sunday.

"Religion has been around for a very long time, and if we rush to try to push for results and want to immediately 'liberate' people from the influence of religion, then it will have the opposite effect and push people in the opposite direction."

About half of China's religious followers are Christians or Muslims, with the other half Buddhists or Daoists, he said, admitting the real total number of believers was probably much higher than the official estimate of 100 million.

Wang did not address specific issues, such as what happens after the exiled spiritual head of Tibetan Buddhism the Dalai Lama dies, testy relations with the Vatican or controls on Muslims in the restive Xinjiang region in the west.

Rights groups say that despite a constitutional guarantee of freedom of belief, the government exercises tight control, especially over Tibetans, Uighur Muslims in Xinjiang and Christians, many of whom worship in underground churches.

Beijing also takes a hard line on what it calls "evil cults", like banned spiritual group Falun Gong, who it accuses of spreading dangerous superstition.

Still, while religion was savagely repressed during the chaos of the 1966–76 Cultural Revolution, the government has taken a much more relaxed approach since embarking on landmark economic reforms some three decades ago.

The ruling Communist Party, which values stability above all else, has even tried to co-opt religion in recent years as a force for social harmony in a country where few believe in communism any more.

China had avoided the religious extremism which happened in some places with the collapse of the Soviet Union or the religious problems seen with immigrants in Europe and the United States, Wang added, something to be proud of.

Still, China could not rest on its laurels.

"Religion basically upholds peace, reconciliation and harmony . . . and can play its role in society," Wang said.

"But due to various complex factors, religion can become a lure for unrest and antagonism. Looking at the state of religion in the world today, we must be very clear on this point."

Written Statement Submitted to the United Nations Human Rights Council

Mouvement contre le Racisme et pour l'Amitié entre les Peuples (MRAP)

In 2012 a French humanitarian organization, the Movement Against Racism and for Friendship Among Peoples (MRAP), submitted the following viewpoint, a report on conditions in Tibet, to the United Nations Human Rights Council (UNHRC). The UN published it on behalf of the International Campaign for Tibet, intending to discuss the report at the council's 2012 meeting in Switzerland where, perhaps, it could influence official UN policy. This viewpoint claims that Tibetans continue to suffer from a variety of human rights abuses carried out by the Chinese government. These abuses range from discriminatory laws regarding education and unemployment, to religious discrimination, to violent crackdowns against dissident monks and other protestors. The authors also note that economic development in Tibet has not been shared equally; ethnic Chinese, or Han, have benefitted the most, instead of the local population. MRAP was first formed in 1949 and continues to fight against discrimination both within France and around the world.

Adapted from Written Statement Submitted by the Mouvement contre le Racisme et pour l'Amitié entre les Peuples (MRAP), a Non-Governmental Organization on the Roster, February 10, 2012, UN Human Rights Council Publishes Written Statement on Discrimination in Tibet, International Campaign for Tibet, savetibet.org. Cengage Learning is responsible for the adaptation.

Against the chronic human rights in Tibet, Chinese discriminatory rhetoric and practices have only intensified with the Tibetan people continuing their demand for human rights and fundamental freedoms. The 21 Tibetan self-immolation protests since February 2009 are directly related to the discrimination and heavy handed tack that Chinese authorities engage in to govern Tibet.

The Committee on the Elimination of Racial Discrimination's 2009 concluding observation on the People's Republic of China listed a number of concerns regarding the PRC's management of discrimination, and unfortunately, few of those concerns have been assuaged by any policy changes, on the contrary the Committee's recommendations have been disregarded with alarming regularity. The Chinese government has created an atmosphere of discrimination, with human rights abuses extending well past the CERD's mandate. Because PRC lacks any substantial anti-discrimination laws its failure to protect the rights of the Tibetan people is unsurprising.

Discriminatory Policies and Laws

CERD commended the PRC's adoption of laws on Regional Ethnic Autonomy (REAL) for minority autonomous areas, however the impact of these laws and the authorities' tendency to disregard them have negatively affected Tibetans. Although the PRC's autonomy laws require that the governmental leaders of Tibetan autonomous areas must be Tibetan, there is no such requirement for the position that holds real authority at all levels of the system: Communist Party Secretary. Beginning with Zhang Jingwu (1951–1965), every Communist Party Secretary in the Tibet Autonomous Region but one—Wu Jingua of the Yi minority—has been Chinese.

While REAL calls for schools in Tibet to teach the Tibetan language, in many of these schools Tibetan is not the medium of education and is instead often only taught as a single course during the day. A joint intervention on October 22, 2010 by the

Modern China's Ethnic Minorities

The vast majority of the people living in China belong to the mainstream Han ethnicity. But about 8.5 percent of the nation's overall population (1.2 billion people) belong to ethnic minority groups.

China's government recognizes 56 different ethnic minority groups. A number of them are quite large, such as the Zhang peoples who live in southern China and the Manchu people in the northern region known historically as Manchuria. Other groups not only are large but also maintain cultures and ways of life quite different from that of the mainstream Chinese. In addition to the Tibetans these groups include the Muslim Uighurs who have a language and history connected to Turkey, as well as the Mongols who also speak a Turkish-related tongue.

China's official position is that ethnic minorities share the same legal rights and privileges as all Chinese people including freedom of speech, press, and association. China also claims to respect the traditional languages, religions, and other customs of these groups, asserting that rights to observe them are protected. Members of these groups, the government asserts, should meanwhile obey Chinese laws and maintain loyalty to the state.

Ethnic activists, however, often claim that minorities are under threat despite these official protections. Strong pressure exists, for example, to use Mandarin Chinese as a primary language rather than, say, Tibetan or Uighur. Inability to speak Mandarin might make it difficult for minorities to deal with Chinese officials, or to access education or jobs. Many parts of China that have historically been dominated by these minorities are seeing increasing Han Chinese settlement, and many of these newcomers serve as government officials or in other powerful positions.

Special Rapporteur on the right to education, the Independent Expert in the field of cultural rights, the Special Rapporteur on Contemporary forms of racism, racial discrimination, xenophobia and related intolerance and the Independent Expert on minority issues during the 17th Session of the UNHRC raised concerns over such restrictions to teaching Tibetan language. This intervention came after protests in Qinghai and Beijing by Tibetan students and teachers opposed to new restrictions to Tibetan language education.

Discriminatory Law Enforcement

CERD had concerns surrounding the Chinese authorities' excessive use of force following the 2008 demonstrations that swept across the Tibetan Plateau. The report noted the "disproportionate use of force against ethnic Tibetans . . . and the important number of their detentions" and requested their fair trials and humane treatment in custody. Prison sentences for Tibetans detained for participating in the 2008 demonstrations were harsh, and the welfare of these detainees concerned Special Procedures mandate-holders of the Council.

Concern remains for monks from Labrang Monastery in Sangchu (Xiahe) county, Kanlho (Gannan) Tibetan Autonomous Prefecture, Gansu province, who participated in the March 2008 protests as well as those who spoke out during a government sponsored media visit to the monastery in April 2008. Following the March 14 and 15, 2008 protests at Labrang Monastery numerous Labrang monks were detained and many severely tortured. One monk who had participated in the March 2008 protest, Tsultrim Gyatso, was sentenced to life and another, Thabkhe Gyatso, to 15 years in prison. The authorities did not inform family members of the trial and denied them access to the monks during the year-long pre-trial period.

Like the Labrang monks, many of the Tibetans detained following the March 2008 protests were denied basic provisions for fair trials under Chinese law. Many Tibetans, including two who were executed, were denied the right to be represented by the lawyer of their choice, and several lawyers were threatened with disbarment if they attempted to represent detained Tibetans. Such discriminatory law enforcement and prosecution was noted as a concern by CERD.

While these cases of discrimination took place soon after the March 2008 protests, more pressing are the concerns over the Tibetans currently facing harsh penalties in the current atmosphere of discriminatory repression in Tibet.

Three monks at Kirti Monastery in Ngaba (Aba) Tibetan and Qiang Autonomous Prefecture in Sichuan province were imprisoned for between 10 and 13 years for "intentional homicide" following the death of a young monk called Phuntsog who self-immolated on 16 March 2011. There is no evidence that the three monks had any involvement in Phuntsog's solitary act of self-immolation or subsequent death, other than possibly seeking to protect him from further harm before he died in the hospital. Reports from Tibetans in exile in the region indicated that due legal process was not followed in the three cases, with the Tibetans unable to choose their own lawyers and the whereabouts of all three prisoners being withheld from their families upon detention.

On January 24, 2012 Chinese police opened fire on a crowd of Tibetan protesters in Serthar (Chinese: Seda) in Sichuan province, killing one and injuring others. Such disproportionate use of force—firing into a crowd of unarmed protesters—was also used in Drango (Chinese: Luhuo) county town in Kardze (Chinese: Ganzi) Tibetan Autonomous Prefecture, Sichuan on January 23, 2012 where three Tibetans were killed and many more injured, as well as in Ngaba on January 27, 2012 where one Tibetan was killed.

Chinese officials have now locked down several Tibetan towns in present-day Sichuan and Qinghai provinces with heavy-handed military controls imposed in three counties: Serthar, Kardze, and Draggo. Lhasa, the Tibetan capital, Dartsedo (Kangding) and Lithang (Chinese: Litang) are also on full-scale military alert.

Discrimination on the Basis of Religious Belief
In 2009 CERD expressed its concern for the free practice of religion among ethnic minorities. China continues to place

Tibetan Buddhist monks protest near the Labrang monastery in Gansu province, China, on March 14, 2008. Many monks were detained and tortured as a result of this demonstration. © Mark Ralston/AFP/Getty Images.

restrictions and hindrances on the free practice of religious freedom. In a November 2011 joint statement, Special Rapporteur on the Freedom of Religion and Belief, Mr. Heiner Bielefeldt stated that the Chinese government's restrictive policies "Not only curtail the right to freedom of religion or belief, but further exacerbate the existing tensions, and are counterproductive."

In 2007 the Chinese government passed "management measures for the reincarnation of living Buddhas in Tibetan Buddhism" which declares that Tibetan Buddhist reincarnates must have state approval. The Dalai Lama has spoken regarding his own reincarnation, explaining that only he will determine how he will reincarnate and that the Atheistic CCP has no say in such matters. For years the CCP has carried out an all out media offensive against the Dalai Lama, vilifying him and accusing him of 'splittism.' These attacks against the Dalai Lama have reached beyond official pronouncements to "patriotic education" campaigns in Tibetan monasteries that require monks and nuns to publicly denounce the Dalai Lama. Such an action is in direct conflict with their monastic vows and is anathema to Tibetans who revere the Dalai Lama as their spiritual leader. The 21 self-immolations since February 2009 are directly linked to these discriminatory policies. The dying words of many of those who self-immolated called for the Dalai Lama's return to Tibet.

Discrimination Through Economic Development

While CERD warned that "economic growth in minority regions, ipso facto, is not tantamount to equal enjoyment of economic, social and cultural rights in accordance with article 5(e) of the Convention," the rapid economic development in Tibet has not been equally enjoyed.

Chinese authorities have undertaken development projects which include the rebuilding of the earthquake-destroyed-Kyegu (Chinese: Yushu), which has caused protest by local Tibetans opposing the government's plan for the reconstruction; and nomad settlement policies on the plateau which, in the name of modernization, relocate Tibetan nomads into pre-fabricated housing communities, separate from the sustainable livelihoods they had practiced for centuries.

In-migration fed by the 2007 construction of the Golmud-Lhasa rail line has had deleterious effects on Tibetans in part because of the discriminatory hiring practices of private and public entities operating in Tibet, many of which offer positions to "Han only" or offer the same work to Tibetans for less pay.

It has emerged that job advertisements in Tibet, both online or notices posted in public spaces, show overt discrimination against non-Chinese with Tibetans not even being offered menial, unskilled work in some sectors, or if they are, being offered a wage significantly lower than their Chinese counterparts.

According to different sources, the practice of advertising positions "limited to Han" is also observed in the Inner Mongolia Autonomous Region, Ningxia Hui Autonomous Region and

Xinjiang Uyghur Autonomous Region—referred to by its historical name of East Turkistan by many Uyghurs in the People's Republic of China (PRC).

Recommendation

MRAP urges the Special Rapporteur on Contemporary forms of racism, racial discrimination, xenophobia and related intolerance to closely monitor the situation faced by Tibetans, Uyghurs and Mongolians and seek a fact-finding mission to the People's Republic of China.

Hollywood Celebrates the Year of Tibet

Tim Cornwell

In the following viewpoint, British journalist Tim Cornwell examines Tibet's influence among many celebrities—a fascination that peaked in the 1990s but continues into the twenty-first century. According to Cornwell, the most active of these celebrities include actor Richard Gere (who has been barred from traveling to China or Tibet due to his outspoken views), Hollywood personality Goldie Hawn, and the late musician Adam Yauch of the hip-hop group Beastie Boys. Others who have spoken out include Brad Pitt, Harrison Ford, and Sharon Stone. Meanwhile, Cornwell asserts, Hollywood produced a number of films sympathetic to the Tibetan cause in the 1990s. These included Kundun, *directed by Academy Award-winner Martin Scorsese;* Seven Years in Tibet, *which starred Pitt as a German in exile there during the World War II years; and Bernardo Bertolucci's* Little Buddha. *The last of these intertwined the historical story of the original Buddha, set some 2,500 years ago, with a modern search for the reincarnation of a living Tibetan Buddha. One candidate in the search was a young boy living in Seattle, Washington. As Cornwell reports, some Tibetan activists, for their part, hoped that all this attention*

Tim Cornwell, "Hollywood Celebrates the Year of Tibet," *The Independent*, March 23, 1997. Copyright © 1997 by The Independent. All rights reserved. Reproduced by permission.

from the world of entertainment might make their cause much more widely known. Cornwell is a writer for a number of British publications focusing on American subjects and concerns.

The Dalai Lama began a six-day visit to Taiwan this weekend in the face of angry protests from China. "Splittists" is how Peking refers both to the Tibetan god-king and Taiwanese President Lee Teng-hui, accusing them of agitating for independence. "The Chinese communists have repeatedly used the Dalai Lama's visit to attack us," President Lee said this week. "We should not be afraid of the Chinese communists' intimidation."

A bigger nightmare for Peking, however, may be threatened with the visit of the Dalai Lama to Los Angeles this summer. His early years are now the subject of two big-budget studio films, both scheduled for release by Christmas. On his last trip to the States stars as diverse as Harrison Ford and Shirley Maclaine queued to meet him.

A Hollywood love affair with Tibet and Tibetan Buddhism, several years in the making, promises to reach its climax in 1997—dubbed "Year of Tibet in the Movies" by hopeful human rights campaigners. The films—with their World War II era settings, and thematic echoes of both *The Last Emperor* and *The English Patient*—are feeding hope in the Tibetan exile community that Hollywood's clout will help the Tibetan cause.

"It will have tremendous popular impact," predicts Tenzin Tethong, a former long-time adviser to the Dalai Lama, who was hired as a consultant on *Seven Years in Tibet*. The film, directed by Jean-Jacques Annaud (*The Bear, The Name of the Rose, Quest for Fire*), stars no less a heart-throb than Brad Pitt (*Seven*), playing an Austrian mountaineer who flees a British prisoner of war camp for the Tibetan court. "A lot of young people all over the world, including large numbers of Chinese, will be watching this movie for sure," Mr Tethong says. "It will be banned in China, and what gets banned gets seen, some times more."

His work on the film included correcting speech patterns and mannerisms that were not Tibetan, and minor adjustments to a scene or two where people wore the wrong ceremonial hats. *Seven Years in Tibet* recently completed filming in the Andes. The production moved to South America, it is reported, after intervention by Chinese officials persuaded the Indian government to block filming there.

The film comes with the usual Hollywood mixture of high fakery and authenticity at any cost. As well as recreating throne rooms in the Dalai Lama's 1,000-room palace, Annaud imported a herd of yaks, and some 150 Tibetan extras from India. Bolivians dressed as Tibetans were used to fill out the crowds. The cast includes British actor David Thewlis (*Naked*), and the Dalai Lama's sister, Jetsun Pema, playing his mother. The film is based on the true story of Austrian Heinrich Harrer, who befriended the Dalai Lama.

The Chinese Government has made no bones of its irritation. It placed the cast and crew on a black list for Tibetan visas, though Annaud is said to have secretly shot footage in the country. Last year, Disney was warned that the company's business in China could suffer if a rival film, *Kundun*, directed by Martin Scorsese, went ahead. Disney refused to back down and 59 Hollywood figures signed an open letter protesting against censorship.

Kundun, filmed in Morocco, is based on the autobiography of the Dalai Lama, and is now set for release on Christmas Day. Using a cast of unknown Tibetan actors, with a slow-moving plot and ending with leaving Chinese-occupied Tibet for India in 1959, it hardly carries the sex appeal of Brad Pitt. It was written however, by Melissa Mathison, screenwriter for *ET* and wife of Harrison Ford.

Western fascination with the mysticism and mystery of Tibet has a long history. But in Hollywood it dates back to 1937 and Frank Capra's film of *Lost Horizon*. In a romantic adventure, four westerners are rescued from a plane crash by monks, and taken

Actor Richard Gere (left) and his wife, supermodel Cindy Crawford, pose with the Dalai Lama at a 1993 gala benefit in Beverly Hills, California. © AP Images/Reed Saxon.

to the blissful valley of Shangri-La to meet Lamas hundreds of years old.

But it was in the 1990s that Tibetan Buddhism began to draw prominent members of the Hollywood set. Oliver Stone helped import Tibetan Lamas to California, and a number of Tibetan film projects got under way. A low-budget independent film, *The Wind Horse*, recently completed filming, promising the "urgent, contemporary story of an aspiring Tibetan pop singer". By contrast, one of Hollywood's most macho action heroes, Steven Seagal, also commissioned a script based on the CIA's ill-fated operations in Katmandu, Nepal. A "Tibetan Western" is the description by those who have read it.

There are now 21 Tibetan centres, or dharmas, in Los Angeles, most established in the last two or three years. The star names involved run from serious committed Buddhists, like Richard Gere, who famously denounced China from the Oscar stage in 1993, to others more generally supportive of the Tibetan cause. Tina Turner is a Japanese Buddhist practitioner. Oliver Stone is said to have a Buddhist shrine in his home. Goldie Hawn is a big supporter of the Dalai Lama. Sharon Stone is on the board of the American Himalayan Foundation.

Los Angeles based British film-maker Martin Wassell, who has made documentaries on Tibet and "His Holiness", cites the image of the Dalai Lama in a Microsoft commercial as evidence that things Tibetan have entered the popular mainstream—50 years after the Chinese invasion and the oppression that followed. The Tibetan Buddhist belief system, centred on realising one's human potential, appeals to a culture keen on therapy, he said. Hollywood also "loves a good cause, especially where there's an underdog involved. The injustice of this holocaust that the world has chosen to ignore, it resonates with Hollywood's tinsel heart".

Some Tibetans Object to Hollywood Views of Their Culture

Barbara Stewart

As celebrities and filmmakers grew fascinated with the subject of Tibet in the 1990s, some Tibetans became concerned that their films provided a view of Tibet that was not accurate. In the following viewpoint, journalist Barbara Stewart examines these opinions. She reports that some Tibetan expatriates find Hollywood's version of Tibet too romanticized and serious with too much emphasis on religion and spirituality. The root of this misconception, one of Stewart's interviewees suggests, was the 1930s film Lost Horizon, *which depicted the then-mostly unknown Tibet as Shangri-La—a lost hidden world of great mystery, wisdom, and peace. The viewpoint argues that many in the West have clung to the myth of Tibet as a lost Shangri-La. Tibetans themselves claim that, instead, Tibetans are just as ordinary as other people, with the same qualities of humor, playfulness, courage, and even anger. Some hope that films could be made that reflect this reality. Stewart has worked as a journalist for such newspapers as the* New York Times *and* Boston Globe.

Over the past decade, there have been three lavish Hollywood movies about Tibet and its Buddhist monks, several docu-

Barbara Stewart, "Tibet (Hold the Shangri-la)," *New York Times*, March 19, 2000. Reproduced by permission.

mentaries and a few lower-budget independent films, the latest of which is *The Cup*, about a monastery in India whose young Tibetan monks are swept up in a passion for the World Cup soccer final.

To Tibetans expatriates, Hollywood's portrayals of Tibet—like Bernardo Bertolucci's *Little Buddha* (1993) and Martin Scorsese's *Kundun* (1997)—are overflowing with exaggerated reverence, with heavy-handed depictions of Tibetans, especially Tibetan monks, as solemn, holy and kind instead of as ordinary people who quarrel and joke around.

Jamyang Norbu, a Tibetan immigrant and writer living in Tennessee, said: "In the West, the response to Tibetan culture is so worshipful and romantic. There are elements in Tibetan culture that have all this magical, medieval stuff that Westerners love. The New Age thing. The Tibetan thing has style—the color, the costumes. To a great extent, we exist only in the imagination of Western fantasists."

A More Realistic View of Monks

Considering the Hollywood versions of Tibet and Buddhist monks, Mr. Norbu considers *The Cup*, which opened in late January [2000], to be a fresh breeze. In it young monks break the rules, sneaking out at night and snickering over Victoria's Secret catalogues and snapping wisecracks during kitchen duty. "It has a sense of fun and a sense of reality," Mr. Norbu said. "It's not trying to make some huge statement, but it's truth-telling. There's a sense of sadness about it, deliberately underplayed."

The director of *The Cup*, Khyentse Norbu, a high-ranking Buddhist lama from Bhutan (who is no relation to Jamyang Norbu), knows the foibles of young monks well, having taught in monasteries in Bhutan and India for years.

"The romantic idea should stop now," Khyentse Norbu said. "In the West, people have higher expectations and see Tibetans as holy and high—people who don't eat and sleep. Sooner or later, they're going to be disappointed. I'm trying to demystify Tibetans."

To his mind, *Kundun*, about the current Dalai Lama's early life in Lhasa, is the best of the Hollywood takes on Tibet. It recreated the grandeur of the Potala Palace, the former seat of the Dalai Lama, as well as some of the political machinations of the Chinese government, and included bloody scenes of the Chinese destruction.

The myth of a magical Tibet inhabited by otherworldly holy men was first popularized by *Lost Horizon*, the Depression-era hit that starred Ronald Colman. In it, some Englishmen are downed in a plane crash in the Himalayas. They are rescued by residents of Shangri-La, a place of constant serenity, where wise lamas offer the visitors proper cups of tea and urbane philosophical conversation—in English. Campy as it now seems, *Lost Horizon* struck a deep chord in the West, creating a myth that present-day Tibetans living in the West are still grappling with.

"Shangri-La was one of the West's most powerful utopian images," said Orville Schell, whose book, *Virtual Tibet: Searching for Shangri-La From the Himalayas to Hollywood* (Henry Holt), is due out this spring. "It was Tibet but not too Tibet—awfully clean, with libraries filled with the great works of Europe."

Over the last 10 years, the Dalai Lama's books have appeared regularly on best-seller lists, numerous Tibetan lamas have taught Buddhist philosophy and meditation in the West and Hollywood has become entranced with Tibet. But, according to Mr. Schell, as well as to several Tibetan filmmakers and film buffs, all three Hollywood extravaganzas—including the 1997 *Seven Years in Tibet*—bore traces of the daydreams of *Lost Horizon*. The movies seem to view Tibetans and Buddhist monks through a veil of awe—as a devout Catholic might look at the Pope. "Slavishly reverent," said Mr. Schell.

For Thupten Tsering, the co-director of *Windhorse*, a 1999 low-budget movie about a family damaged by the Chinese regime that was shot surreptitiously in Tibet, the reverence and exaggerated respect of the Hollywood productions have an undercurrent that it is a bit insulting. "People assume that if you are

Kundun, *a film that depicts the early life of the current Dalai Lama, drew some criticism for its misrepresentations of Tibetan culture.* © AP Images/HO-Mario Tursi.

Tibetan, you are peaceful and polite and smiley," he said. "They are imposing this Shangri-La fantasy myth on Tibetans. They see Tibetans as cute, sweet, warmhearted. I tell people, when you cut me, I bleed just like you."

Along with *Windhorse* and *The Cup*, another realistic portrayal was a low-budget 1998 documentary, *The Saltmen of Tibet*, about nomads and their annual three-month trek with their yaks to remote salt lakes for the bags of salt that provide their living. Both *The Cup* and *The Saltmen of Tibet* have a subtle undercurrent of mourning for the loss of their culture and country. And both show Tibetans as people who laugh and joke readily and have a sharp wit.

Gesar Mukpo, a 26-year-old Tibetan-American and an aspiring filmmaker, resents the Hollywood stereotype of the holiness of the Tibetans. "How many Italian movies do you see that aren't about the Mafia?" he said. "I don't want every Tibetan movie to be about holy people. I'd like to make a Tibetan action movie. It would be interesting to see ordinary Tibetans flourishing back in warring times."

Tibetan Action Heroes?

The enthusiastic reception of *The Cup* is encouraging, he said. Perhaps the time will soon be ripe for Mr. Mukpo to attempt a film about the warriors of Tibet, a kind of Tibetan *Braveheart*. Another idea he has is a film about a tulku—a person who is thought to be a saint in a previous life—who rebels against the monastic life.

During the '70s Jamyang Norbu lived in Darjeeling, India, where his family escaped to when he was a child, and he remembers how shocked Western tourists were when they saw Tibetan teenagers with guitars playing Jimi Hendrix songs.

"They want to insist that our religion is everything," he said. "When Tibetans get together, we drink a little too much, we sing songs—Bob Dylan, maybe—and they don't like that."

He said he hopes that *The Cup* will help rid Hollywood of its visions of Tibetans as wise mystics, and open the doors to a broader view of Tibet and Tibetan Buddhism that can convey the depth of the Tibetans' religious views, their sadness over exile and the Chinese occupation of their land, and their day-to-day humor. At the very least, he said, he could then go to Hollywood movies about Tibet without fear of embarrassment over their solemn pieties. The low point, for him, was a scene in *Seven Years in Tibet*, in which a frowning monk scolds the Brad Pitt character for carelessly killing some earthworms. 'Those earthworms could have been your mother,'" said Mr. Norbu, repeating the lines of the movie in a voice heavy with sarcasm. "Please, no more hurting!"

"It was like *Saturday Night Live*," said Mr. Norbu. "Every Tibetan I know shudders over that scene."

Tibet's Culture Itself Offers Examples of Persecution and Oppression

Sorrel Neuss

China has justified its takeover of Tibet by claiming that it has provided the Tibetan people greater opportunity and freedom, bringing elements of a modern infrastructure, such as clean water and electricity, to what had been a rather backward area. In the following viewpoint, British writer Sorrel Neuss helps to illustrate those claims. She suggests that until quite recently, certainly in the centuries before the Chinese takeover, the vast majority of Tibet's people consisted of agricultural serfs, workers bound to their lands by powerful aristocrats and monasteries. But since the end of the rebellion in 1959 that sent the Dalai Lama into exile, Neuss writes, ordinary Tibetans enjoy greater personal freedom and access to education, and she notes that life spans have doubled. Neuss does not downplay alleged Chinese abuses, especially against dissidents and exiles. But she tries to provide a broader perspective on Tibet than is generally acknowledged in the outside world. Neuss is a journalist who has worked in China and Tibet as well as elsewhere in Asia.

Sexual abuse in monasteries and oppressive feudalism in traditional Tibetan society has been factored out of the argument against China's occupation, oversimplifying it.

Sorrel Neuss, "What We Don't Hear About Tibet," *The Guardian*, February 11, 2009. Reproduced by permission.

Han Chinese guards deliberately obstruct the pilgrim route through Lhasa [Tibet's capital] to the holy Jokhang temple by sipping tea at strategically placed tables in the middle of the road. In front of the Potala, the Dalai Lama's former seat of power, an imposing guarded concrete square glorifies China's occupation.

Tibet seems like a celestial paradise held in chains, but the West's tendency to romanticise the country's Buddhist culture has distorted our view. Popular belief is that under the Dalai Lama, Tibetans lived contentedly in a spiritual non-violent culture, uncorrupted by lust or greed: but in reality society was far more brutal than that vision.

Last December [2008], Ye Xiaowen, head of China's administration for religious affairs, published a piece in the state-run *China Daily* newspaper that, although propaganda, rings true. "History clearly reveals that the old Tibet was not the Shangri-La that many imagine," he wrote "but a society under a system of feudal serfdom."

Until 1959, when China cracked down on Tibetan rebels and the Dalai Lama fled to northern India, around 98% of the population was enslaved in serfdom [in which farm laborers are bound to the land and not entirely free]. Drepung monastery, on the outskirts of Lhasa, was one of the world's largest landowners with 185 manors, 25,000 serfs, 300 pastures, and 16,000 herdsmen. High-ranking lamas and secular landowners imposed crippling taxes, forced boys into monastic slavery and pilfered most of the country's wealth—torturing disobedient serfs by gouging out their eyes or severing their hamstrings.

Tashi Tsering, now an English professor at Lhasa University is representative of Tibetans that do not see China's occupation as worse tyranny. He was taken from his family near Drepung at 13 and forced into the Dalai Lama's personal dance troupe. Beaten by his teachers, Tsering put up with rape by a well-connected monk in exchange for protection. In his autobiography, *The Struggle for Modern Tibet*, Tsering writes that China brought long-awaited hope when [it] laid claim to Tibet in 1950.

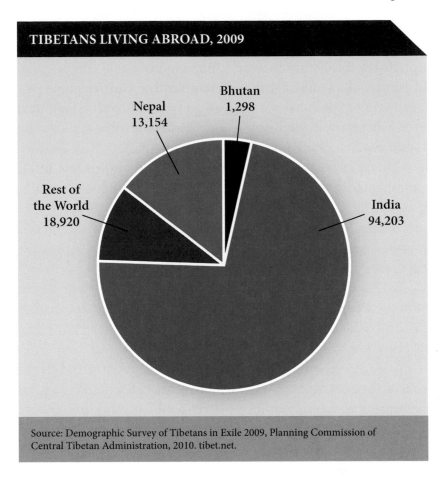

TIBETANS LIVING ABROAD, 2009

Nepal
13,154

Bhutan
1,298

Rest of
the World
18,920

India
94,203

Source: Demographic Survey of Tibetans in Exile 2009, Planning Commission of Central Tibetan Administration, 2010. tibet.net.

The Chinese Were Liberators

After studying at the University of Washington, Tsering returned to Chinese-occupied Tibet in 1964, convinced that the country could modernise effectively by cooperating with the Chinese. Denounced during the Cultural Revolution, arrested in 1967 to spend six years in prison and labour camps, he still maintains that Mao Tse-Tung liberated his people.

Caught between a system reminiscent of medieval Europe and a colonial force that brought forced collectivisation and similar human rights abuses, Tibet moved from one oppressive regime to another.

During the 1990s, Tibetans suspected of harbouring nationalist tendencies were arrested and imprisoned and in 2006, Romanian climbers witnessed Chinese guards shooting a group of refugees headed for the Nepalese border. China's abhorrent treatment of "political subversives" has rightly spurned a global Free Tibet movement, diminishing the benefits that it did bring to society.

After 1959, it abolished slavery, serfdom and unfair taxes. Creating thousands of jobs through new infrastructure projects, it built Tibet's first hospitals and opened schools in every major village, bringing education to the masses. Clean water was pumped into the main towns and villages and the average life expectancy has almost doubled since 1950, to 60.

Even so, in 2001 the Dalai Lama said: "Tibet, materially, is very, very backward. Spiritually it is quite rich. But spirituality can't fill our stomachs."

Freedom for Tibet is not simply a case of liberation from China and the reinstatement of traditional values. Around 70 per cent of the population lives below the poverty line and enhanced spirituality alone will not improve economic conditions. Poverty is not quaint no matter how colourful the culture and the Tibet question is one that should be addressed from a rational, rather than an idealised viewpoint.

Nearby Bhutan, which has a similar Buddhist culture that it tried to preserve by banning television until 1999 and limiting foreign visitors, only held its first democratic elections in 2007. The Dalai Lama now promotes democracy, but Tibet may well have looked worse than it does today if the old order had been left to its own devices.

CHAPTER 3

Personal Narratives

Chapter Exercises

1. **Writing Prompt**

   Imagine that you are a Tibetan who knows other Tibetans who have gone into exile and that you are thinking about going into exile yourself. Write a one-page journal entry describing your thoughts and feelings.

2. **Group Activity**

   Divide into groups and come up with five interview questions that could be used to build oral histories describing the experiences of exiled Tibetans.

Growing Up in Tibet's Years of Crisis

Jetsun Pema with Gilles van Grasdorff

The following viewpoint comes from a memoir by Jetsun Pema, the Dalai Lama's sister and therefore a member of Tibet's aristocracy. She recalls some of the events of the year 1959, when she attended private school in Darjeeling, India. As a schoolgirl, she heard news of a Tibetan rebellion that had been crushed by Chinese troops and of the Dalai Lama's subsequent exile to India. What followed were intense emotions and changes in her day-to-day existence, although the Dalai Lama encouraged her to continue her education. In her later years Jetsun Pema served as a member of the Tibetan government-in-exile and ultimately as president of the Tibetan Children's Villages. In this capacity she has been honored as the "Mother of Tibet."

17March was particularly important at Loreto [the author's Catholic school in Darjeeling, India]. The nuns were mostly from Ireland, and so each year they celebrated St Patrick's Day. The occasion was marked by a basketball match. However, that year I did not feel much enthusiasm for practising for my final competition: Gyalo Thondup and Lobsang Samten

Jetsun Pema with Gilles van Grasdorff, *Tibet: My Story, An Autobiography*. Rockport, MA: Element, 1996, pp. 62–66. Reproduced by permission.

[relatives] had joined us in Darjeeling, bringing very alarming news with them.

The Indian and British newspapers led with the events in Tibet on their front pages. We learnt that there had been an uprising on 10 March 1959 in Lhasa. The most worrying rumours were circulating. Some said that the Dalai Lama was a prisoner of the Chinese, others that there was no news of His Holiness and his family. The BBC also reported on the subject. When I went to see my brother Gyalo Thondup at the weekend, there was a tremendous coming and going at the house. Faces were marked by anxiety. In spite of the attempts to reassure us, my niece and I knew that something very serious was happening. I was frightened for Amala, my sister and her husband, and for Tendzin Choegyal and, of course, His Holiness. I trembled at the idea that their lives might be in danger. I was also worried for the Tibetans that I knew personally, and for our people who were going through the most terrible times. However, anything I was imagining was a far cry from the reality of the tragedy being played out beyond the Himalayas.

In Loreto, the nuns collected the newspapers for us. Morning and evening, they asked everyone to pray for 'Pema's family'. Everyone at the school therefore knew about our tragedy. In spite of everything, I could not hold back my tears when I heard the announcement of the firing of guns and cannons by Communist troops—tears of revolt and despair.

Important News

Three long weeks went by. Suddenly the news spread like wild-fire. The Dalai Lama and his entourage had succeeded in crossing the Indian frontier and had reached Tezpur [a border town]. Gyalo Thondup had left a few days earlier to meet his brother. In Tezpur hundreds of journalists and photographers welcomed the spiritual and temporal leader of the Tibetans.

My sister-in-law, who had remained in Darjeeling, came to Loreto to tell us the happy news. My niece, nephew and I were allowed to listen to the BBC, which had interrupted its programmes to broadcast newsflashes from Tezpur. My relief was complete when at last I heard the journalist announce that the Dalai Lama and all his family were out of danger. They were going to Mussoorie, Northern India, a resort in the Himalayan foothills, by special train. The radio then announced a message from the Indian prime minister to His Holiness the Dalai Lama: 'Upon your safe and sound arrival on Indian territory, my colleagues and I welcome you. We are happy to offer you, your family and your entourage, the facilities necessary to reside in India. Our people, who hold you in profound veneration, will without doubt show the traditional respect due to your person.'

The mother superior of Loreto gave us a day off. My niece, nephew and I were able to accompany Diki Dolkar [an assistant] to Siliguri where the train carrying His Holiness was due to arrive. On the way we passed the Tibetans living in the region of Darjeeling and Kalimpong, eager to welcome the Dalai Lama.

When the coach entered the station an enormous crowd surged on to the platform. Everyone showed deep veneration on this exceptional day. The Indian people also expressed their rejection of the expansionist politics the Chinese Communists had been practising for the last ten years.

We had great difficulty in making our way to the platform. Suddenly a shout of joy went up. The door of the carriage opened, revealing bodyguards and then, finally, His Holiness, who seemed to have been terribly affected by events and had lost a lot of weight. His Holiness seemed exhausted and anxious. The few paces that separated us seemed to take an eternity to cover. I offered him a khata [scarf], received his blessing and was then literally thrown into the train by the bodyguards. At last I was able to embrace Amala [Mother] whom I had missed so much during these difficult times, and then my sister and brothers. We were all together again at last, for the first time since 1956, three years earlier.

Of course, my niece, nephew and I did not want to go back to Loreto, and it took some strong persuasion on Amala's part to make us accept that we must return to boarding school. We therefore left for Darjeeling two hours later, with the assurance that we would see all the family during the holidays. Two hours . . . two hours of intense emotion, of tears and questionings. What fate awaited our families? What was going to happen to His Holiness, and to the Tibetans who had remained behind in our country? The questions came from all sides, but no one had the time to give us replies, still less to explain the situation to us. In fact, we were simply living the happy conclusion to a long month of fears and anxieties.

I was, however, able to imagine how terrible it must have been to leave Lhasa. My family was exhausted and completely dejected. They had fled without luggage and had worn the same clothes for several weeks. Diki Dolkar had brought a few clothes and a little food. Indeed, we no longer owned anything, but I was so pleased to find them alive that nothing else seemed very important. Nevertheless, at that precise moment, I realized that we were starting a new life: a life of exile as political refugees.

That evening and all the following ones, I had great difficulty in getting to sleep. Images continuously rose up into my mind: the house in Lhasa, our games in the gardens with the servants and their children, school, the kites. I was very worried about His Holiness and my mother. However, Amala remained confident in the future and an imminent return to Tibet. As for His Holiness, he also showed enormous courage. He believed, and still does, that a solution exists for all difficulties. He also, with his strong belief in justice and faith, placed his hope in the support of the Indian government and other nations.

A First Airplane Trip

A little later we had four days holiday and my brother Gyalo Thondup came to collect my niece, nephew and myself. Darjeeling–New Delhi was to be our first journey in an airplane, a flight during which we experienced wonderful sensations. However, when we arrived in the capital, it was so hot that we had only one thing in mind: to leave that furnace as fast as possible. The journey to Mussoorie was made by car.

My family had fairly good lodgings. His Holiness occupied two rooms in a fine house that belonged to Birla, a rich Indian industrialist. Amala and my youngest brother shared a bedroom, and so did my sister and her husband. His Holiness's secretaries and advisers lived in two further rooms. Amala and my sister looked after the cooking, helped by one of our servants who, in spite of her great age, had managed to follow my family into exile. The Indian government had also placed several servants at our disposal, and they were responsible for the smooth running of the house.

Gyalo Thondup rushed around the house. Concerned for His Holiness's comfort as well as for that of the rest of the family, he continually asked them if they needed anything. In fact, they needed everything. At meal times, Amala complained that she did not have enough cups or saucers and that she needed spoons. My brother would go out for several hours and return laden like a mule. If my sister said that she no longer had a dress or shirt, Gyalo Thondup would go out once again. I could imagine Tsering Dolma's unhappiness as she was very attached to her clothes and now had nothing. Sometimes she discreetly wiped away a tear.

Mussoorie was at this time a holiday resort for Indians fleeing the suffocating heat of the capital. When my brother was unable to find everything he needed in the town, he prepared a long list and went to New Delhi for his purchases.

I spent only four days with my family. Even though sadness was visible on their faces, they all reacted in a positive manner. They refused to become demoralized by the situation but, on the contrary, gave much thought to the future of the Tibetan people, such as whether the United Nations should be contacted, or whether help should be solicited from elsewhere in the world.

As soon as he arrived in Mussoorie, His Holiness decided to open a school to teach English to 50 young Tibetans. Mr and

Mrs Taring gave the lessons. This was the beginning of the first Tibetan school in exile. This wonderful couple continued working for the Tibetan children for almost three decades, and came to be considered as Pala and Amala [father and mother] to hundreds of students who passed through this school. Many of their students later held important positions in the Tibetan government and in the Tibetan settlements scattered around India.

One evening my mother and sister asked my niece and nephew and me to join them in the drawing room. I learnt that my long-time companions were to continue their studies in Mussoorie and that I was to return alone to Loreto. They insisted on the usefulness of this training. The Dalai Lama was also convinced that a modern education could help serve the Tibetan cause. Confronted with the sight of my family so penniless, I regretted that I was still only a simple schoolgirl. I felt that I was both powerless and at the sme time invested with an important mission: to finish my studies as fast and as well as I could.

Years in a Prison Camp

Adhe Tapontsang

During the 1950s, 1960s, and 1970s, it was common for China's new Communist leaders to send to prison camps those who actively disagreed with the policies and practices of the new regime. In these camps both political dissidents and members of ethnic minority groups would receive "re-education" while also being subjected to hard labor and other harsh conditions. In the following viewpoint, Adhe Tapontsang, a Tibetan woman arrested after the failed uprising of 1959, recalls her first experiences in one of these prison camps. The camp, a former Tibetan Buddhist monastery, was filled with prisoners of various origins who were sometimes put to work in full view of people outside the walls. The author remembers the poor food, overcrowded conditions, and heavy-handed efforts at "re-education" carried out by Chinese officials. She was able to take comfort, however, in her deep Buddhist faith as well as the continued safety of the Dalai Lama, then in exile in India. After her final release in 1985, Adhe Tapontsang left for Dharamsala, India, the center of the Tibetan exile movement.

Adhe Tapontsang as told to Joy Blakeslee, excerpts from *Ama Adhe: The Voice That Remembers: The Heroic Story of a Woman's Fight to Free Tibet.* Copyright © 1997 by Joy Blakeslee and Adhe Tapontsang. Reprinted with the permission of The Permissions Company, Inc. on behalf of Wisdom Publications, www.wisdompubs.org.

The truck pulled into the courtyard of Ngachoe monastery. The ransacked monastery, which had been one of the largest in the area, was now a prison and had been completely sealed off from the public. We could see that many of its rooms were being used as prison cells. Approximately sixty monastic prisoners, including learned *geshes* (monks who have received the highest degree possible within the monastic educational system), incarnate lamas, and ordinary monks were detained in what used to be the assembly hall. Male lay [nonmonastic] prisoners were held in rooms surrounding the courtyard where the sacred cham dances once had been performed.

Upon our arrival, we were each given one piece of steamed dough and a cup of tea. Then we were brought into the prison office to be registered. As evening fell, I was taken to a cell occupied by a group of women. . . . no bedding was supplied, although some of the inmates had managed to carry a few things with them. Unfortunately, when I was arrested, my only possession was the clothing that I was wearing. My chuba [Tibetan-style dress] itself was my bed. I used the sleeve for a pillow. As I lay down, I looked around me.

The room, about nine by fifteen feet, served as a cell for sixteen women. Eight women lay on each side, having about one and a half feet of space to themselves in which to sleep. In the center of the room was a wooden toilet pot. Whether one wanted to urinate or defecate, there was no privacy. Many prisoners, being unaccustomed to the poor food, had diarrhea; and the smell was very intense. As I tried to sleep, I was overwhelmed with the all-too-familiar stench of close confinement. As I settled into my small, cold space that first night, images of the last twenty-four hours [travelling to the prison] came before me, but weariness soon overcame my scattered thoughts and I fell into a deep sleep.

Forced Labor

The following morning and every morning thereafter, the prisoners were awakened at seven. At eight, we were given a small cup of watery gruel; and at nine, we were gathered together in the courtyard and then escorted by guards to work in lines of two. We generally worked for four hours and then were given something to eat. After lunch, most of the prison guards rested for an hour, and the prisoners worked for another four hours. My first assignment was to carry stones for the construction of new cells. The monastery was not large enough to accommodate the hundreds of prisoners being sent there. There were about eight hundred men detained at Ngachoe, and women lay prisoners numbered about three hundred. Altogether, about 1,200 Tibetans were being detained there in midsummer of 1959.

We carried the stones from the stone quarry to the construction sites at the prison, perhaps one kilometer. The stones were transported by means of a wooden plank that had several holes for straps and a wooden base on which up to four stones would be laid. A strap held them in place, and there were other straps for one's arms. My first day at the quarry I had no idea how such an implement was to be used. The first time I tried to use it, I put it on upside down. Immediately, the guards began to shout at me. They ran to where I was standing and began to beat me. Several struck me in the face, demanding, "Why did you put it on upside down? There must be a reason for doing this. What are you trying to do?" I replied, "I've never seen this before. I've never done such work, so how could I know?"

I was relatively young and healthy, so the work was not too much of a hardship for me; but I was devastated by something else: each day we watched elderly lamas being forced to carry heavy stones as they were kicked and beaten with rifle butts.

Cultural Attacks

Since the advent of Buddhism, Tibetans have understood that there is much more to life than obtaining one's daily bread. We have striven to comprehend the unity of life, to pray for the upliftment of all, and to fill our lives with acts of good merit. Our lamas took strict vows and devoted themselves to serious study and contemplation of the truths espoused by the Lord Buddha. They spent years memorizing the basic principles of Buddhism and then learned to put the precepts into practice—mentally, through dialectical debate, and spiritually, through years of meditation. Now these lamas, so revered in our society, were being treated in such a lowly way. It greatly upset me and the other prisoners, for we could do nothing to stop it.

The Tibetan population outside the prison witnessed this also, and they cried at seeing their lamas being treated in this manner. While carrying stones in the prison, I could look outside and see people who were free. I then remembered my childhood and all the happy times I'd had with my family and wondered, Why? Why were we undergoing this now? I cried and constantly wondered how such sufferings and atrocities could be happening in this world. What was the purpose of such cruelty? They had invaded our land and taken away our possessions, our family members, our way of life, our religion, all our hopes and dreams, and then were forcing us to work as slaves for them. Yet, they were saying that we were evil for opposing them. What could we do?

In order to survive these sufferings, my cellmates and I felt that there was no other means than to pray to His Holiness and to the deities. In the nights, I could only pray. . . .

Ideological Training

We all dreaded the nightly two-hour reeducation meetings during which prisoners were prosecuted for various reasons: perhaps a prisoner was caught saying some mantras, or someone was not working diligently. Often there were "statistics meetings" during which the officials mentioned the names of different kinds of bombs they had acquired. They said, "America does not have these things. Only we have them." We found such statements difficult to believe, as we had heard something of the amazing devastation of the atomic bombs dropped on Japan. The Chinese also told us that their military divisions had "achieved this" or "installed that." They would say, "We have found a new source of petrol, and it is running in abundance like water. All is in abundance. The reserve is in abundance."

They also said, "We have discovered so many different kinds of medicine in Tibet. We want medicinal herbs, and your people want money. Our medicines are so well known that all over the world people are pleading to us for them." We did not believe that they were giving money to our people. They recounted how much China was earning in exports and how many orders they were receiving from different countries in the world.

Basically, the purpose of those meetings was to make the prisoners believe that in every respect—politically, economically, militarily—China under the Communist Party had no equal in the world. The impression was given that no other country could compete with the Chinese. These were the basic points of indoctrination.

Helpless to Protest

The warden of the prison, Zhang Su-dui, was one of the rare Communist officials who spoke fluent Tibetan. He was the son of a Guomindang [anti-Communist] porter from Sichuan, but somehow, after the Communist occupation, he had risen to a position of senior officer. He was in his late twenties and had a round face and staring eyes. He took an interest in young and attractive women prisoners. They were often called by him to clean his rooms and do his laundry. During this work, he also repeatedly raped them.

I was one of these women. Three others were also selected for this duty: Nangtso Wangmo, from Lingkarshe, a region bordering Lithang district, and Dolkar and Yangchen from Chatring. We were called in rotation and raped. As a precaution against us getting pregnant, he forced us to drink musk water immediately after intercourse. If we resisted, we were threatened with harsh punishments, even death. We could only obey and keep silent.

For us, this was an ultimate degradation. We had lost everything; we didn't know the fate of our families and our children; our people had been turned into a work force of slaves—but this was one of the most difficult things we had to bear. We were powerless. We came to hate Zhang, who was always rough and crude and would purposely say things to try to make us feel ashamed and hopeless. Although such activity was officially illegal according to the Communists' military rules, there was no one to come to our defense. There was no question of reporting the matter to higher authorities, for the only result would have been that we would be locked in our cells without food. Moreover, Zhang Sudui was himself the authority.

There was no way to console ourselves. We regarded the times when each of us was called as a sort of execution. After one was called, the rest cried over the deplorable situation, and we tried to console each other as best as we could. After some time, Zhang grew concerned that we might somehow speak out. We noticed that if he saw us stealing vegetables, he ignored the situation, looking the other way. These were the things we thought of as we sat in the nightly classes in which they explained to us that we had been liberated by the world's most advanced and powerful government.

[Lama] Chomphel Gyamtso Rinpoche, in trying to comfort me, often said, "You must always remember that His Holiness the Dalai Lama has been able to escape. Even though we are suffering very dark times, it will not be possible for them to destroy our religion and culture. Ultimately, the doctrine of Tibetan Buddhism will prevail."

A Chinese Man Challenges His Own Understanding of History and Geography

Harry Wu

Although it was not part of China in the first half of the twentieth century, Tibet has been considered part of the larger Chinese empire at other points in a long history going back thousands of years. After China's Communists secured control over the country in 1949, they again claimed that Tibet was part of a "greater China" which should be united once again. They used this thinking to help justify their occupation of Tibet beginning in 1950. The following viewpoint was written by Harry Wu, a pro-democracy dissident who spent years in a Chinese labor camp before moving to the United States. Wu describes how, as a young man, he never doubted that Tibet is part of China but, as an adult, his research convinced him that Tibet is an entirely separate region with its own distinct history and customs. He suggests that, rather than liberating the Tibetans since 1950, the Chinese Communists have simply brought oppression. Wu hopes that the Tibetan independence effort might help spark pro-democracy efforts in China. Wu's books include Laogai: The Chinese Gulag *and* Troublemaker.

When [Chinese premier] Deng Xiaoping came to power in the late 1970s he put forward his now well-known policies calling for the modernization of China's industry, agriculture, national defense, and science and technology. These became known as the Four Modernizations. Then, in the winter of 1979, a young Beijing electrician named Wei Jingsheng expressed dissatisfaction with the idea and advanced the notion that China needed a *fifth* modernization, namely, political modernization, the main component of which was democracy. For this "crime" he was locked up for several years in Beijing, and then transferred to the Thirteenth Laogai Farm, a forced labor camp in Amdo, where the majority of the residents are Tibetans. We Chinese know the area as Qinghai Province. Wei was confined there for four and a half years. Later, on the basis of this experience, he wrote his well-known letter to Deng Xiaoping regarding the patriarch's policy on Tibet.

In 1991 I went to China from the United States to investigate and expose the darkness of China's gulag [prison camp system]. During that investigation I made a special point of visiting the Thirteenth Laogai Farm. I went there not only because Wei Jingsheng had once been jailed there but also because the camp was located in the Qaidam Basin. This part of Qinghai, along with the Tarim Basin of Xinjiang, is called "China's Siberia." Like the outlying, desolate Siberia of Russia, the two northwestern regions became natural prisons where about one million convicts have been jailed by the Beijing authorities since the 1950s. Many among them are "felony" political prisoners.

From Xining, the capital of Qinghai Province, I went to the west toward the Thirteenth Laogai Camp, crossing over the mountain [known to Tibetans as Ninda La and to us Chinese as] Riyue. When I reached the crest of Mt. Riyue, beside a tent for travelers to rest I found a stone tablet on which was engraved a bit of history. China's Princess Wen Cheng's marriage to the Tibetan king, Songsten Gampo, had taken place in the year 641, and Princess Wen Cheng had crossed these mountains on her way to Tibet.

"Upon arriving here, Princess Wen Cheng performed a farewell ceremony that included a bath, a fast, and a kowtow to the East—in farewell to her country and family. After the ceremony, the princess changed to Tibetan dress and went to Tibet escorted by a squad of guards of the Tibetan king." History, as recorded on the tablet, shows that the marriage of Princess Wen Cheng and the Tibetan king Songsten Gampo was not the marriage of an emperor's daughter to a general of the emperor's subordinate province; rather, it was a political marriage between two equal countries. As I read this tablet, I realized I was standing on the old border which had demarcated two sovereign nations, Tibet and China.

Patriotic Ideas

This was quite different from what I had learned about the history of Tibet and Sino-Tibetan relations since my childhood. Both the Chinese Republican government before 1949 and the Chinese Communist government after 1949 had told me that our country was composed of five nationalities: Han, Manchu, Mongolian, Hui (Chinese Muslim), and Tibetan; we had a vast territory of 9.6 million square kilometers and a rich civilization of five thousand years. This empire, which included what is now the People's Republic of Mongolia, was engraved on my mind in the shape of a mulberry leaf.

I considered myself a patriotic young man. I used to recite patriotic poems by the poet Lu You. When I had occasion to visit the city of Hangzhou, I would take pictures of the tablet on which was engraved the famous patriotic General Yue Fei's phrase of loyalty to our country. So when China recognized the independence of "Outer Mongolia" in 1950, I might as well have been hit by a cudgel. It was difficult for me to accept the separation; I saw it as a piece cut off from the beautiful mulberry leaf. Then only a teenager, I believed that the separation of Mongolia from China was a national shame and a plot by the Soviet imperialists.

In the 1950s, when I attended college in Beijing, I learned that Mongolia had been altogether independent since 1924,

Harry Wu displays his book on Chinese prisons during a 2009 human rights hearing at the US House of Representatives. © Mandel Ngan/AFP/Getty Images.

though China had not accepted the fact. It was only after Mao [Zedong] established Communist China that, under the pressure of the Soviet Union, China reluctantly recognized the People's Republic of Mongolia. In fact, to this day, the Republic of China on Taiwan has never recognized "Outer Mongolia" as an independent country, even though the People's Republic of Mongolia has long been a member of the United Nations and is recognized by almost all nations around the world. Maps of China printed in Taiwan still show my great mulberry leaf.

Growing Doubts

Before coming to the United States in 1985, I had never doubted that Tibet was part of China, and I had never heard of the Tibetans' separatist movement. When I learned, soon after my arrival, that

Tibetans were seeking independence, my first response was that it might be another imperialist plot, with someone else wanting to cut off another piece of the mulberry leaf. When I heard more about the independence movement, I began to wonder if Tibet really is part of China, so I began to read books on the subject. I learned that the real history of Tibet is quite different from what I was taught by the two Chinese governments.

Even *The Atlas of Chinese History Maps*, published by the Chinese Social Science Institute in Beijing, clearly shows that Tibet was an independent country and never a part of China at least before 1280, when the Mongols established what we Chinese call the Yuan dynasty. The Beijing government and most of the Chinese people use the Yuan dynasty's rule over Tibet as Historical "proof" of China's sovereignty over Tibet. It is obvious that the Yuan dynasty was a Mongol empire that included most Asian countries such as China, Korea, Vietnam, as well as Tibet. After the demise of the Yuan dynasty, the Ming dynasty reestablished the Chinese Empire. However, its authority was largely limited to China proper; it had little or no control over the Northwest, the Northeast, or Tibet. The lands to the north and northeast of China were inhabited by the Manchu people, who had an alliance with the Mongols, and the Tibetans also joined in this political and religious alliance. When the alliance, dominated by the Manchus, overthrew the Ming dynasty and established the Qing, that dynasty became suzerain over Mongolia and Tibet [ruling from 1644 to 1911].

The Revolution of 1911 toppled the Manchu rulers and established the Republic of China. Ironically, while recognizing the abolition of the Qing dynasty, all of China's rulers after the 1911 Revolution, including the founding father of the Republic, Sun Yat-sen, presidents of the Republic of China Chiang Kai-shek, Chiang Ching-kuo, and Lee Teng-hui, and leaders of the People's Republic of China Mao Zedong and Deng Xiaoping, had no doubt that they had inherited the territory of the Qing dynasty and that Tibet was a part of China, as it had been during the Qing dynasty. They have also used slogans, such as "republicanism" for the five nationalities and "autonomy" for minority ethnic groups, to justify the retention of the Qing empire's domain.

In reality, during the Republican period, China had endured separatist warlord regimes, as well as the Japanese invasion and the civil war. The central government was too weak to handle such a vast territory. Therefore, during the period from 1911 to 1950, Tibet was in fact an independent country. But many Chinese historians have accepted the current rulers' stand and have even helped the authorities to instill in the populace a twisted version of history, imbued with Han chauvinism.

Two Separate Countries

However intoxicated the Chinese may be with the idea of a vast Great China, unbiased history books provide us with a different story, at least concerning Tibet; that is, until the Communists took over Tibet, the country had had its own political system, religion, currency, taxation, law, army, and government. Because of its special geographic position and culture, Tibet had little association with the outside world except for some contact with its neighboring countries. The Qing court rarely, if at all, interfered in Tibet's politics, economy, judiciary, and army. Indeed, its respect for Tibet's religion and its material support had greatly helped to stabilize the Tibetan government and to promote a friendly relationship between China and Tibet.

Unfortunately, in 1950 Tibet was occupied by the Chinese Communist army. Communists regard the "liberation of all human beings" as their duty; of course Tibet was part of this responsibility, especially in view of Tibet's "backward culture." Nowhere have Communists allowed religion to flourish. This was to be especially true in Tibet, for Lamaist Buddhism was deemed to be evil.

In his poetry Mao Zedong likened himself to the Tang and Qing emperors (who "unified" China), and his aim was to establish a huge, homogeneous Chinese Empire. Now, since the

Communists claimed to have "liberated" Tibetans, they have had to devise a rationale for this "liberation." So the Beijing authorities retroactively condemned Tibet as a barbaric, slave society that had been in need of liberation. True, some aspects of the old Tibetan system were unreasonable, such as the integration of politics and religion and violations of human rights. But has anyone the right to destroy a society by force? Moreover, what has socialism actually done for the Tibetans? Consider the following:

- In Tibet's entire history, never have so many people fled into exile as under the Communists.
- In all of Tibetan history, never has there been such severe destruction of their religion as there is today—six thousand temples were destroyed and hundreds of thousands of monks and nuns were forced to resume secular lives.
- On Tibetan land, never have there been so many Chinese in control of all political power and the country's economic lifeblood;
- Never have there been on Tibetan soil so many prisons and of such enormous size and forced labor camps—as many as twelve according to one investigation.
- Never have there been so many soldiers and police in Tibet as there are today.

While we Chinese are fighting for democracy, freedom, and human rights in our homeland, we must be aware that Tibetan people have the same right to fight for their freedom, democracy, and human rights. Even if Tibet had never been an independent country, the Tibetans would still have the right to choose their own political system, religion, and lifestyle. The descendants of the French in Quebec are not being denounced as "splittists" simply because they seek independence from Canada. I do not believe that a great number of Chinese people would like to live on the Tibet Plateau. Most of them who have gone to Tibet were coerced or deceived. I think any Chinese currently in Tibet should go home, and they should not be used by the government as tools of nationalism.

The Chinese Communist dictatorship is like a plate composed of Beijing, Shanghai, Tibet, Ningxia, Sichuan, and the other provinces and regions. Here live Hans, Manchus, Mongols, Huis, and Tibetans. The breakup of any part of the plate could lead the entire plate to crash. Actually, in terms of the economy, culture, and population of the People's Republic, Tibet does not comprise much of the Communist plate. Nonetheless the Tibetans' fight for freedom and democracy could be a catalyst effecting the disintegration of the entire Communist dictatorship. Isn't that just what our Chinese brothers and sisters need—to smash the shackles of communism?

An American Doctor Tells of Atrocities in Tibet

Blake Kerr

In the following viewpoint, an American doctor and frequent visitor to Tibet, Blake Kerr, reports on trips to the region he has taken since 1987. He describes witnessing various acts of violence including Chinese attacks on protesters. These atrocities, he says, also included forced abortions and infanticide committed on the basis of China's "one-child" policy largely forbidding women from having more than one baby in order to slow population growth. As Kerr writes, he later presented much of this information to a Spanish court seeking to hold responsible two former Chinese leaders for crimes against humanity. Although the original case against these leaders, Jiang Zemin and Li Peng, was shelved in 2010, Spanish courts continue to be a forum in which Tibetan activists and their supporters try to establish legal standing and accountability on behalf of the larger Tibetan cause. Kerr is the author of Sky Burial: An Eyewitness Account of China's Brutal Crackdown in Tibet.

Based on the principle of Universal Jurisdiction, Chinese officials including the former prime minister and president, Li Peng and Jiang Zemin, are facing criminal charges by Spain's

National Court for crimes against humanity in Tibet from 1971 to 1998. On December 12, 2011, I presented medical testimony to this court concerning egregious crimes that I witnessed and investigated in Tibet.

The Spanish National court has ruled that China's policies in Tibet of torture, forced abortions, sterilizations, infanticide, disappearances, arbitrary execution, religious persecution, racial discrimination, and population transfer all present a prima facie [at first sight] case for genocide.

On October 1st, 1987, after traveling as a tourist to the Tibetan capital of Lhasa, I documented 12 deaths when Chinese police massacred unarmed Tibetans demonstrating for independence. There were no medicines for a ten-year-old boy who died in my arms after being shot by a sniper, a 23-year-old man who had been shot through the heart, or a mother pouring water onto her 16-year-old son's unresponsive lips. The boy had been beaten to death, with a shovel, inside the police station.

When Chinese soldiers took injured Tibetans from Chinese hospitals to prisons, I snuck out to treat wounded Tibetans hiding in their homes and monasteries.

Birth Control Teams Devastate Tibetan Communities

Besides the victims of torture, I encountered something worse. A Tibetan woman named Kunsang explained to me that she was six months pregnant with her first child when she was ordered to the People's Hospital. Once inside, a Chinese doctor insisted that she have an operation to save her life and injected her abdomen. Kunsang heard her baby cry twice: when her son's head appeared, and when the doctor gave a lethal injection in the soft spot on his forehead. The next day Kunsang was sterilized. On examination, her scar was consistent with sterilization.

From 1991 to 1999, I returned to Tibet three times to conduct on-site investigations. My interviews with physicians at hospitals across Tibet, first-hand Tibetan accounts of coerced abortion, sterilization and infanticide at Chinese-run hospitals in Tibet, as well as Tibetan refugee accounts in India and Nepal, indicate that these practices were prevalent throughout the 1990s.

China's National Family Planning Policy operated on a pressure continuum. Tibetan women were informed that it is technically legal to have a second child, but it is "best" to have only one, like the Chinese. Chinese law required that both Chinese and Tibetan women must be married and have permission to give birth. Women with unauthorized pregnancies faced coercive abortion, sterilization and economic sanctions.

China's birth control teams operated in hospitals in cities and towns throughout Tibet; mobile teams traveled to remote villages and nomad areas. Both teams had monetary incentives to induce abortions during the first trimester by D&C [dilation and curettage method], and during the second and third trimesters by injections of Levanor into the uterus.

The more procedures the doctors performed, the more money they received from the Chinese government.

Two monks from the Amdo region of Tibet described to me what they had seen when a mobile birth control team erected a tent next to their monastery in 1987. The villagers were informed that all women had to report to the tent for abortions and sterilizations. Women who refused were taken by force and operated on. Women nine months pregnant "had their babies taken out."

During the two weeks the tent stood in the village, the monks stated, "We saw many girls crying, heard their screams as they waited for their turn to go into the tent, and saw the growing pile of fetuses build outside the tent, which smelled horrible." As a physician, I found the monks' description of coerced abortions and sterilizations, women's post-surgical scars and other medical details to be credible.

My testimony to the Spanish National Court details the systematic violence against unarmed Tibetan civilians by Chinese security forces that I witnessed in 1987, the torture of Tibetan political prisoners, and the widespread, state-sponsored forced abortions and sterilizations of Tibetan women through the 1990s.

While the Spanish National Court seeks justice for Tibetans suffering under China's military occupation, it also strengthens the principle that there must be no impunity for genocide or other grave crimes committed anywhere, regardless of how powerful the perpetrators may be.

Glossary

Amdo: The northern portion of the Tibetan plateau; formerly part of Tibet, it is now divided among several Chinese provinces.

Bhutan: A small Buddhist nation in the Himalayas that is the destination of some Tibetan exiles.

Bodhisattva: A soul that, according to a number of Buddhist sects, has achieved enlightenment or is close to it, meaning that the soul has reached or is near reaching nirvana, a state of permanent bliss. Many bodhisattvas remain active in the world to help others achieve enlightenment.

Bon: A shamanistic religion that predates Buddhism in Tibet and still has numerous followers.

Cold War: The ideological and diplomatic conflict between democracy (as represented by the United States and its allies) and communism (as represented by powers including China and Soviet Russia that dominated the second half of the twentieth century).

Cultural Revolution: An attempted overturning of Chinese society and culture carried out by China's leaders from 1966 to 1976. Many ethnic minorities, such as Tibetans, became targets for further persecution.

Dalai Lama: The spiritual and, until 2011, political leader of Tibet. Considered a living Buddha, or enlightened soul.

Dharamsala: A town in Himachal Pradesh province in northern India that has become the chief center for Tibetan exiles and the home of the Tibetan Central Administration.

Great Leap Forward: China's attempt at rapid agricultural and industrial development from 1958 to 1962. Many Tibetans were turned into forced laborers or imprisoned.

Han: The majority ethnic group in China, making up over 90 percent of the population.

Lhasa: The traditional capital of Tibet, now the administrative center of the Tibet Autonomous Region of China.

Nepal: A small nation in the Himalayas between China and India and the home of many Tibetan exiles.

Panchen Lama: The second-highest ranking figure in Tibetan Buddhism after the Dalai Lama and also an important figure politically. The identity of the current Panchen Lama is under dispute; the Chinese government and the Dalai Lama back two different candidates.

People's Liberation Army (PLA): China's armed forces. The PLA carried out the initial occupation of Tibet in the 1950s.

People's Republic of China (PRC): The official name of China's current governing regime, in power since 1949.

Potala Palace: The former residence of the Dalai Lama in Lhasa and an important spiritual center in Tibetan Buddhism.

Tibet Autonomous Region: A province of the People's Republic of China comprising much, but not all, of historical Tibet. It is also known as Xizang.

Tibetan Central Administration: The organization providing a form of democratic governance to Tibetans in exile as well as a focus for international interest in the Tibetan cause. It is not an officially recognized government in exile and does not seek to act as such.

Tibetan National Uprising Day: A holiday celebrated by many Tibetan exiles and designed to commemorate the March 10, 1959, uprising that sent the Dalai Lama into exile.

Tibetan Parliament in Exile: The governing body at the center of the Tibetan Central Administration.

Tibetan Plateau: A vast, high-altitude region in Central Asia, part of which is historical Tibet. Known metaphorically as the "roof of the world," it is isolated from other regions by high mountain ranges such as the Himalayas.

Organizations to Contact

The editors have compiled the following list of organizations concerned with the issues debated in this book. The descriptions are derived from materials provided by the organizations. All have publications or information available for interested readers. The list was compiled on the date of publication of the present volume; the information provided here may change. Be aware that many organizations take several weeks or longer to respond to inquiries, so allow as much time as possible.

Amnesty International
5 Penn Plaza, 14th floor
New York, NY, 10001
(212) 807-8400 • fax: (212) 463-9193
e-mail: aimember@aiusa.org
website: www.amnestyusa.org

Amnesty International is a global organization seeking to advocate everywhere on behalf of what it terms internationally recognized human rights. Its basis is the Universal Declaration of Human Rights as well as other international human rights standards. Each year it publishes a report on its work and its concerns throughout the world.

Human Rights Watch
350 Fifth Ave., 34th floor
New York, NY 10118-3299
(212) 290-4700, (212) 736-1300
e-mail: hrwnyc@hrw.org
website: www.hrw.org

Founded in 1978, this nongovernmental organization conducts systematic investigations of human rights abuses in countries around the world. It publishes many books and reports on specific countries and issues, as well as annual reports and other articles. Its website includes numerous discussions of human rights and international justice issues.

International Campaign for Tibet
1825 Jefferson Place NW
Washington, DC 20036
(202) 785-1515 • fax: (202)785-4343
e-mail: info@savetibet.org
website: savetibet.org

The International Campaign for Tibet monitors human rights conditions in Tibet, advocates on behalf of imprisoned Tibetans, and seeks to foster communications between Tibetan and Chinese authorities. It also works with organizations and individuals around the world to gain humanitarian and development aid. The organization's website offers general information about Tibet and its issues, as well as news and reports on its current campaigns.

International Tibet Network
c/o Tibet Society UK
Unit 9, 139 Fonthill Road
London N4 3H5, United Kingdom
e-mail: itsn@tibetnetwork.org
website: www.tibetnetwork.org

An umbrella organization for some 180 groups around the world involved in pro-Tibet causes, the International Tibet Network works to enhance communication and cooperation among these groups. Its hope is to give the greater Tibetan cause more power and presence. The organization's website offers resources to find groups advocating for Tibet and resources for these groups around the world to work together. The website also hosts news articles and links to other relevant websites.

Montreal Institute for Genocide and Human Rights Studies
Concordia University
1455 De Maisonneuve Blvd. West
Montreal, Quebec, H3G 1M8 Canada
(514) 848-2424 ext 5729 or 2404 • fax: (514) 848-4538
website: http://migs.concordia.ca

MIGS, founded in 1986, monitors native language media for early warning signs of genocide in countries deemed to be at risk of mass atrocities. The institute houses the Will to Intervene (W2I) Project, a research initiative focused on the prevention of genocide and other mass atrocity crimes. The institute also collects and disseminates research on the historical origins of mass killings and provides comprehensive links to this and other research materials on its website. The website also provides numerous links to other websites focused on genocide and related issues, as well as specialized sites organized by nation, region, or case.

STAND/United to End Genocide
1100 17th Street NW, Suite 500
Washington, DC 20036
(202) 556-2100
e-mail: info@standnow.org
website: www.standnow.org

STAND is the student-led division of United to End Genocide (formerly Genocide Intervention Network). STAND envisions a world in which the global community is willing and able to protect civilians from genocide and mass atrocities. In order to empower individuals and communities with the tools to prevent and stop genocide, STAND recommends activities from engaging government representatives to hosting fundraisers, and it has more than 1,000 student chapters at colleges and high schools. While maintaining many documents online regarding genocide, STAND provides a plan to promote action as well as education.

Students for a Free Tibet
602 E. 14th Street, 2nd Floor
New York, NY 10009
(212) 358-0071 • fax (212) 358-1771
e-mail: info@studentsforafreetibet.org
website: www.studentsforafreetibet.org

Students for a Free Tibet is an organization of young people around the world divided into mostly national chapters. Members work with Tibetans on behalf of Tibetan causes and try to both raise awareness and train future student leaders. The website provides an archive of press releases and a list of action steps for one to get involved in the Tibetan cause.

The Tibet Fund
241 E. 32nd Street
New York, NY 10016
(212) 213-5011 • fax (212) 213-1219
e-mail: info@tibetfund.org
website: www.tibetfund.org

The Tibet Fund seeks to preserve Tibetan identity and culture both within Tibet and around the world. It works for and provides funding for health services, education, cultural preservation, and economic development. The website details the programs the Tibet Fund has underway and provides an opportunity to sponsor a Tibetan in need.

Tibetan Center for Human Rights and Democracy
Narthang Building
Gangsheng Kyishong
Dharmasala (HP)-176215, India
website: www.tchrd.org

Based in India but staffed and run by Tibetans, the Tibetan Center for Human Rights and Democracy monitors human rights issues and engages in outreach and education among both exiled Tibetans and the population in general. The center publishes annual reports and reports on specific issues, all of which are available on the website. Also available on the website are current news stories.

United Human Rights Council (UHRC)
104 N. Belmont Street, Ste. 313
Glendale, CA 91206
(818) 507-1933
website: www.unitedhumanrights.org

The United Human Rights Council (UHRC) is a committee of the Armenian Youth Federation. By means of action on a grassroots level the UHRC works toward exposing and correcting human rights violations of governments worldwide. The UHRC campaigns against violators in an effort to generate awareness through boycotts, community outreach, and education. The UHRC website focuses on the genocides of the twentieth century.

US Tibet Committee
241 E. 32nd Street
New York, NY 10016
(212) 481-3569
e-mail: ustc@ugc.org
website: www.ustibetcommittee.org

The US Tibet Committee provides information on Tibet's history and culture, writings on Tibet, and suggestions for actions that might be taken to improve the lives of exiles as well as enhance the cause of Tibetan freedom. The committee's website hosts a page called, "Fifteen Things You Should Know About Tibet and China," as well as essays and photographs.

List of Primary Source Documents

The editors have compiled the following list of documents that either broadly address genocide and persecution or more narrowly focus on the topic of this volume. The full text of these documents is available from multiple sources in print and online.

Bangkok Declaration, 1993, Final Declaration of the Regional Meeting for Asia of the World Conference on Human Rights

Asian nations declare their support for international agreements and standards for human rights while recognizing the need for respect for the sovereignty and distinct values of independent states.

The Charter of the Tibetan Parliament in Exile

Proposed by the Dalai Lama in 1990, adopted in 1991, and receiving numerous amendments since, the Charter of the Tibetan Parliament in Exile contains the organizing statements and principles for Tibet's exiled leaders. It is intended to provide a model of democracy in action.

Convention Against Torture and Other Cruel, Inhuman, or Degrading Punishment, United Nations, 1974

A treaty adopted by the United Nations General Assembly in 1974 opposing any nation's use of torture, unusually harsh punishment, and unfair imprisonment.

Convention on the Prevention and Punishment of the Crime of Genocide (UN Genocide Convention), United Nations, December 9, 1948

In the aftermath of the Nazi Holocaust against the European Jews and other minorities during World War II, the United Nations developed principles defining genocide as well as measures to prevent it and to punish any perpetrators.

Five Point Peace Plan, 1987

The Dalai Lama's plan to enhance the freedom and autonomy of Tibetan people and to provide a basis for further negotiation with China.

Nobel Peace Prize Acceptance Speech by the Dalai Lama, 1989

In accepting the Nobel Peace Prize in 1989, Tibet's spiritual leader (and political leader at the time) reiterated his call for the freedom of Tibet's people from Chinese control.

Principles of International Law Recognized in the Charter of the Nuremburg Tribunal, United Nations International Law Commission, 1950

After World War II (1939–45) the victorious allies tried surviving leaders of Nazi Germany in the German city of Nuremburg. The proceedings established standards for international law that were affirmed by the United Nations and by later court tests. Among other standards, national leaders can be held responsible for crimes against humanity, which might include "murder, extermination, deportation, enslavement, and other inhuman acts."

Rome Statute of the International Criminal Court, July 17, 1998

The treaty that established the International Criminal Court. It establishes the court's functions, jurisdiction, and structure.

United Nations General Assembly Resolution 96 on the Crime of Genocide, December 11, 1946

A resolution of the United Nations General Assembly that affirms that genocide is a crime under international law.

United Nations General Assembly Resolution on Tibet, 1961

In 1961, in the aftermath of China's crushing of a 1959 rebellion and the departure of the Dalai Lama for exile in India, the United Nations General Assembly asserted the right of Tibet's people to national self-determination.

United States Congressional Resolution on Tibet, 1988

The US Congress calls for increased negotiation between the Dalai Lama and Chinese leaders and for the implementation of democratic procedures in Tibet.

Universal Declaration of Human Rights, United Nations, 1948

Soon after its founding, the United Nations approved this general statement of individual rights it hoped would apply to citizens of all nations.

Whitaker Report on Genocide, 1985

This report addresses the question of the prevention and punishment of the crime of genocide. It calls for the establishment of an international criminal court and a system of universal jurisdiction to ensure that genocide is punished.

White Paper on China's Ethnic Policy and Common Prosperity and Development of all Ethnic Groups, Information Office of the State Council of the People's Republic of China

An official 2009 statement on China's policy of equality concerning ethnic minority groups as well as respect for their religions and traditions.

White Paper on Human Rights in China, Information Office of the State Council of the People's Republic of China

An official statement from 1991 asserting the rights of individuals in the People's Republic as well as the progress of the Chinese state in protecting human rights. It notes China's advancing prosperity as the foundation of human rights.

For Further Research

Books

Phil Borges, *Tibet: Culture on the Edge*. New York: Rizzoli, 2011.

June Campbell, *Traveller in Space: Gender, Identity, and Tibetan Buddhism*. London: Continuum, 2002.

Kenneth Conboy and James Morrison, *The CIA's Secret War in Tibet*. Lawrence: University Press of Kansas, 2002.

Mary Craig, *Tears of Blood: A Cry for Tibet*. Washington, DC: Counterpoint, 1999.

Dalai Lama, *Freedom in Exile: The Autobiography of the Dalai Lama*. New York: HarperPerennial, 2008.

Norbu Dawa, *China's Tibet Policy*. Richmond, Surrey: Curzon Press, 2001.

Melvyn Goldstein, *The Snow Lion and the Dragon: China, Tibet, and the Dalai Lama*. Berkeley: University of California Press, 1997.

Melvyn Goldstein and Gelek Rimpoche, *A History of Modern Tibet, 1913–1951: The Demise of the Lamaist State*. Berkeley: University of California Press, 1989.

Melvyn Goldstein, William Siebenschuh, and Tashi Tsering, *The Struggle for Modern Tibet: The Autobiography of Tashi Tsering*. Armonk, NY: M.E. Sharpe, 1997.

Janet B. Gyatso and Hanna Havnevik, *Women in Tibet*. New York: Columbia University Press, 2005.

Heinrich Harrer. *Return to Tibet*. London: Weidenfeld and Nicolson, 1984.

Heinrich Harrer. *Seven Years in Tibet*. New York: Dutton, 1954.

Pradyumna Karan, *The Changing Face of Tibet: The Impact of Chinese Communist Ideology on the Landscape.* Lexington: University Press of Kentucky, 1976.

Blake Kerr, *Sky Burial: An Eyewitness Account of China's Brutal Crackdown in Tibet.* Chicago: Noble Press, 1993.

John Kenneth Knaus, *Orphans of the Cold War: America and the Tibetan Struggle for Survival.* New York: Public Affairs, 1999.

Roger McCarthy, *Tears of the Lotus: Accounts of Tibetan Resistance to the Chinese Invasion, 1950–1962.* Jefferson, NC: McFarland, 1997.

Chanakya Sen, *Tibet Disappears: A Documentary History of Tibet's International Status, the Great Rebellion and Its Aftermath.* London: Asia Publishing House, 1960.

Sam van Schaik, *Tibet: A History.* New Haven, CT: Yale University Press, 2011.

Anna Louise Strong, *When Serfs Stood Up in Tibet.* San Francisco: Red Sun, 1976.

Thubten Jigme Norbu and Heinrich Harrer, *Tibet is My Country: The Autobiography of Thubten Jigme Norbu, Brother of the Dalai Lama, as Told to Heinrich Harrer.* New York: Dutton, 1961.

Robert A. Thurman, *Why the Dalai Lama Matters: His Act of Truth as the Solution for China, Tibet, and the World.* New York: Atria, 2008.

Periodicals

Ellen Bork, "Tibet's Transition: Will Washington Take a Stand?," *World Affairs*, September–October 2012.

Michael Bristow, "China Confirms Tibetan Executions," BBC News, October 27, 2009.

Allen Carlson, "Moving Past the Wreckage of China's Tibet Policy," *The Diplomat*, March 29, 2013.

Yeshe Choesang, "China Destroys the Ancient Buddhist Symbols of Lhasa City in Tibet," *Tibet Post*, May 9, 2013.

Isaac Stone Fish, "China's Black Hole," *Foreign Policy*, April 26, 2013.

Peter Hessler, "Tibet Through Chinese Eyes," *The Atlantic*, February, 1999.

Andrew Jacobs, "Many Chinese Intellectuals Are Silent Amid a Wave of Tibetan Self-Immolations," *New York Times*, November 9, 2012.

Abraham Lustgarten, "What They're Really Fighting For in Tibet," *Washington Post*, March 23, 2008.

Jethro Mullen, "100th Tibetan Self-Immolates in China, Advocacy Groups Say," CNN, February 14, 2013.

Clarissa Sebag-Montefiore, "Good Lord: In China, Christian Fundamentalists Target Tibetans," *Time*, March 8, 2013.

Elliot Sperling, "Don't Know Much About Tibetan History," *New York Times*, April 13, 2008.

"Tibetan Teens 'Set Themselves on Fire in Western China,'" BBC News, February 20, 2013

Tsering Woeser, "When Tibet Loved China," *Foreign Policy*, January 22, 2011.

Websites

Central Tibetan Administration (www.tibet.net). This website is maintained by the Central Tibetan Administration based in Dharamsala, India. It offers media outreach, explanations of important issues, and statements and perspectives from the Dalai Lama and other officials.

China Tibet Online (www.chinatibet.people.com.cn). Intended to provide a Chinese perspective on Tibetan issues, this website offers news reports, editorial comment, and links to articles and other resources on Tibetan History and Culture.

International Campaign for Tibet (www.savetibet.org). This is a website maintained by the International Campaign for Tibet. It provides updated news reports as well as other resources for students and news organizations.

National Democratic Party for Tibet (www.ndp4tibet.org). This website, run by a political organization pledging support for the Dalai Lama's vision of greater independence for Tibet, offers information on recent Tibetan and Chinese history, publications, and other resources.

Tibet Online (www.tibet.org). This website offers news reports, blogs, informational articles, and links to other resources.

Tibet Oral History Project (www.tibetoralhistory.org). A growing record of interviews of Tibetan elders living in exile, this website also provides photographs and news reports.

Films

Devotion and Defiance: Buddhism and the Struggle for Religious Freedom in Tibet, by Kunga Palmo, 2004. International Campaign for Tibet. Documentary.

Fire Under the Snow, directed by Makoto Sasa, 2008. Imakoko Productions. Documentary.

Red Flag over Tibet, directed by Stephen McMillan and Carmel Travers. 1989. Beyond International. Documentary.

Seven Years in Tibet, directed by Jean-Jacques Annaud, 1997. Mandalay Entertainment. Biography/Drama.

The Shadow Circus: The CIA in Tibet, produced by Ritu Sarin and Tenzing Sonam, 2000. Documentary.

A Song for Tibet, directed by Anne Henderson, 1991. Arcady Films, DLI Productions. Documentary.

Tibet: Cry of the Snow Lion, directed by Tom Piozet, 2002. Earthworks Films. Documentary.

Tibet's Stolen Child, directed by Robin Garthwait, 2001. GG Films. Documentary.

Women of Tibet, directed by Rosemary Rawcliffe, 2007. Frame of Mind Films. Documentary.

Index